Personnel Priorities in Schools Today

Personnel Priorities in Schools Today

Hiring, Supervising, and Evaluating Teachers

Thomas A. Kersten and
Margaret E. Clauson

Published in partnership with the
American Association of School Administrators
ROWMAN & LITTLEFIELD
Lanham • Boulder • New York • London

Published in partnership with the American Association of School Administrators
Published by Rowman & Littlefield
A wholly owned subsidiary of The Rowman & Littlefield Publishing Group, Inc.
4501 Forbes Boulevard, Suite 200, Lanham, Maryland 20706
www.rowman.com

Unit A, Whitacre Mews, 26-34 Stannary Street, London SE11 4AB

British Library Cataloguing in Publication Information Available

Library of Congress Cataloging-in-Publication Data Available

ISBN 978-1-4758-0441-6 (cloth)
ISBN 978-1-4758-0442-3 (pbk.)
ISBN 978-1-4758-0443-0 (electronic)

Contents

Foreword

In over twenty years as a principal, central office administrator, and now superintendent, I have learned what it takes to be a successful school leader. One of the initial lessons I learned was that school administration is a complex endeavor. New administrators are expected to quickly become experts, or at least become well versed, in the myriad of responsibilities. They have to understand how to deal with everything from boilers to buses, the school curriculum to the school carnival, and hot lunches to the latest hot topic. None of these responsibilities, however, is as critical to their personal success as the hiring, supervision, and evaluation of teachers.

When I think back to my earliest days as a teacher, I remember how enthusiastic and eager I was to learn. I assumed that my colleagues were filled with this same optimism as well as the desire to be the very best they could be. Instead, I found that some were excellent, some were "ok," and others . . . well? I questioned why principals ever hired them in the first place! I found myself wondering if anyone was truly paying attention when they hired staff.

When I first became an administrator, I told myself that I would be different. I did not believe that there was any way I would make the same personnel mistakes I had witnessed other administrators make. However, as I look back over my administrative career, even after I became a veteran principal, I realize that I, too, made at least some of the same mistakes. What I did not realize then was just how much I did not know. In retrospect, I could have shortened my personnel management learning curve significantly if I had been more aware of the best practices in personnel management.

As a beginning administrator, I faced two significant challenges. First, no one in the district provided me with a roadmap or even training on the teacher hiring process. In my case, I was left on my own with a large stack of resumes. Somehow, I was expected to wade through the candidates, conduct interviews, and select only the best teachers.

The second challenge was recognizing the absolute value of systematic teacher supervision. Similar to most of my administrative colleagues, I simply handed over the classroom keys and turned new teachers loose to teach. I remember believing that if I hired well, my new teachers would soon develop into well established, veteran professionals as they gained experience. The reality was that I inadvertently left them to sink or swim.

As I gained valuable administrative experience, I began to recognize just how important teacher supervision was to student and school success. I also discovered that my role as a supervisor was much broader that completing a single summative evaluation. Unfortunately, I had limited knowledge and experience to know how best to approach supervision and evaluation. Similar to the hiring process, our district had no well-defined supervision model to follow. We offered a few afternoon sessions for new teachers to review various forms and procedures and we periodically assigned mentors to assist beginning teachers. These mentors often focused simply on management tasks such as operating the copier or accessing the email system.

At that time, the Illinois State Board of Education was just introducing a new state-wide multi-day workshop entitled "Introduction to Evaluation of Certified Staff." All administrators were mandated to complete it. By chance, Tom Kersten was my instructor. During the sessions, he was instrumental in broadening my perspectives on emerging supervisory and teacher evaluation issues and techniques. I started to think much more deeply about teacher supervision and evaluation. Years later, I was fortunate enough to co-teach this same course with Margaret Clauson. These experiences helped me develop the knowledge and skills I needed to be a much more effective administrator.

As I reflect back on my early days as an administrator, I wish that this book, *Personnel Priorities in Schools Today: Hiring, Supervising, and Evaluating Teachers*, had been available to me. Rather than spending years self-discovering much of what I ultimately learned, I could have accelerated my learning and become a much more effective school leader much earlier in my career.

Kersten and Clauson succinctly describe not only the differences between effective supervision and evaluation but provide an interesting historical perspective on how we have come to be where we are today. They provide practical strategies that will help you hire more efficiently and effectively. They offer concrete supervision and teacher evaluation tools that you can use to help teachers develop fully as professionals.

Scott A. Herrmann, EdD
Superintendent
Bannockburn School District 106
Bannockburn, Illinois

Preface

PERSONNEL PRIORITIES IN SCHOOLS TODAY: HIRING,
SUPERVISING, AND EVALUATING TEACHERS

Veteran school administrators understand that quality employees are one of the most important factors in the overall success of the school district. In fact, as a beginning building administrator, I quickly realized the impact both effective and ineffective teachers have on everything from management to school improvement. Education is truly a people-centered business and the quality of employees can make or break an administrator, a school, or a district.

When I stepped into administration as an assistant principal at a Chicago-area middle school, I learned what experienced administrators already knew. Administrators spend most of their time on adult rather than student issues. I initially assumed that teachers would manage students similar to how I did as a teacher. If they had small problems with students, they would deal with them themselves. I thought that experienced teachers would only seek me out for more difficult issues.

Reality soon hit as I witnessed firsthand that not all teachers relate well with students. What surprised me even more was that a certain percentage were actually not student-centered. These faculty members tended to engage in power struggles with students and blame external factors for their lack of success.

At the same time, I had the pleasure of observing the positive impact that strong teachers have not only on the individual students in their classrooms but on the overall school climate and culture. From these initial experiences, I became convinced that if I hired excellent faculty members, my job as an administrator would be much simpler and more satisfying. More importantly, I would have made a significant contribution to student learning.

Consider for a moment administrators you have known over the years. How many have commented that they wished that certain teachers were not on their staff? The reasons poor performing teachers remain employed, of course, are multiple. In some instances poor staff members are inherited from prior administrators who did not place the highest priority on the employment process. They hired marginal teachers rather than do the hard work necessary to find the best. Others were selected from a weak candidate pool to fill a high need position. Some teachers were chosen for political reasons such as knowing a board member or being the relative of an employee or friend.

To complicate matters further, administrators may have retained mediocre performers rather than dismissing them when they were non-tenured. This approach is what I refer to as taking the path of least resistance. Rather than committing the time and energy necessary, they decided it was easier to avoid the work or political complications associated with nonrenewals or dismissal. They may even have convinced their superintendents and themselves that these poor performers were effective just so they did not have to make an unpopular decision.

Avoiding difficult employment decisions and taking the easiest route may initially minimize conflict at the school level. Few teachers are likely to complain when their colleagues are retained. However, the calmness related to the retention of ineffective teachers is usually short lived and even their colleagues become frustrated with their low performance.

Poor performers ultimately become problematic employees by throwing up roadblocks to progress and poisoning the overall school culture. Because of state teacher tenure laws and collective bargaining job protection provisions, dismissal after several years of employment becomes complex, expensive, and extraordinarily time-consuming. You would be wise to remember that if you retain poor teachers, they, in all likelihood, will still be employed long after you leave your position.

As an administrator, you are in a unique position to impact the success of your school for decades to come through the hiring and supervision process. However, you must be a proactive and discriminating leader who is committed to employing and retaining only the most effective teachers. This will require you to develop a thick skin and a discerning eye. This book, *Personnel Priorities in Schools Today: Hiring, Supervising, and Evaluating Teachers*, explores three of the most important personnel responsibilities you have as an administrator: the hiring, supervision, and evaluation of teachers.

Acknowledgments

No book can be well written without the professional assistance of others. This book is no exception. From the early idea stage through final publication, I called on two key individuals to whom I am truly indebted. Each "stepped up to the plate" to assist me without hesitation even though this meant committing a significant amount of personal time. In addition, they provided me with the personal support I needed to see this book through to completion.

Above all, I want thank my wife Beth on whom I have relied heavily. She has been a source of ideas, critical peer reviewer, and manuscript editor. Her constant feedback has helped bring structure and focus to each chapter. She has done so while juggling numerous professional and personal responsibilities as a school district assistant superintendent and new grandmother. I want to thank her for always being there for me.

During the past few years, I have come to rely on my good friend and highly successful superintendent, Nelson Armour, for much assistance. I have always respected and relied on him for his professional knowledge, good judgment, and sound advice. In addition, I have valued his willingness to peer review each of the four books I have written while providing me with reality checks for everything I wrote.

Tom Kersten

The prospect of writing a book is both exciting and overwhelming. I am indebted to Tom Kersten, an accomplished author, for trusting me to be a partner with him. His wisdom, guidance, and support along the way were priceless.

I am grateful for Scott Herrmann's unwavering support, encouragement, and friendship. He is always there to walk alongside me, bringing humor and wisdom that help me to be my very best.

Many of my co-workers, past and present, provided nuggets of information that have been woven throughout this book. I would like to especially acknowledge Katie Lee, Suzanne Goff, and Kelly Hansen for their particular insights.

And, finally, I would not be where I am today without the love and support of my wonderful family. Thank you mom, JP, Jill, Hannah, Andrew, and Alex Clauson! I know my dad is bursting with pride at the thought of me being an author.

Margaret Clauson

ONE

Understanding the Historical Basis of Teacher Supervision and Evaluation

Public school teacher evaluation in the United States is not a recent phenomenon. Some form, albeit very informal, of teacher evaluation has been a function of public education supervision for more than 400 years. However, prior to the mid-twentieth century, school leadership expectations were narrowly focused. Administrators were organizational managers who were expected to manage their schools efficiently. Terms such as instructional leadership or curriculum standards were not yet part of the leadership dialogue (Kersten & Ballenger, 2012).

Today, educational leadership is complex. Being a good manager does not ensure success. Principals, in particular, must be knowledgeable, adept, and skilled leaders who can negotiate political waters while leading school improvement efforts.

One of their primary responsibilities is the supervision and evaluation of teachers. Those who understand the latest trends and best practices will be well positioned to be highly effective supervisors. An important first step is developing an understanding of how supervision and evaluation practices evolved over the past four centuries.

THE EARLY YEARS

As early as the mid-1600s, local community officials were primarily responsible for assessing teacher performance. Teacher evaluation was used by local officials including school boards, community leaders, government officials, and others to control teachers (Baker, 1996). Burke & Krey (2005) describe this evaluation approach as inspection. Evaluators made judgments on how well teachers performed their basic responsibil-

1

ities. Community leaders expected teachers to be good school managers who maintained control of students and met minimum curriculum expectations. Ensuring that students were learning was not a supervisor's responsibility.

During this period, local officials exercised broad supervisory autonomy. They could discipline any teacher as they saw fit. In fact, dismissing a teacher for almost any reason was common practice. Arbitrary dismissals and political hiring were accepted practices. As a result, teachers were truly at-will employees. (Burke & Krey, 2005).

As the industrial revolution movement spread from Britain to the United States in the late 1700s to early 1800s, it cultivated a new perspective on economic growth often referred to as the industrial economy. Over the next 100 years, business interests became very focused on efficiency. It was during this period that the factory system was developed. Under this approach, business consolidated large scale work projects in centralized location (Independence Hall Association, 2013). This movement ultimately impacted public education including teacher supervision throughout the United States.

FOCUS ON EFFICIENCY

By the mid-1800s, public school leaders began to feel the effects of these emerging business practices. As public schools grew in size and complexity, specialized educational roles emerged. Community leaders realized that depending on minimally knowledgeable and unskilled individuals to oversee public schools was insufficient. What were developed were new supervisory roles such as chief administrator and business manager (Tracy, 1995).

These supervisors were required to function as inspectors and ensure some performance consistency. "Lay inspection of the school gave way to professional inspection" (Burke & Krey, 2005, pg. 10). Supervisors were minimally expected to help teachers improve instruction.

By the early 1900s, the efficiency movement began to impact public education. Frederick Taylor (1911) through his publication of *The Principles of Scientific Management* not only influenced business management but indirectly public education. He argued that to increase productivity, businesses needed to simplify jobs and increase management efficiency. He said that to complete this, business leaders should identify the best and most efficient way to accomplish a task and replicate it. He stressed the importance of cooperation, which required managers to interact more directly with workers to improve efficiency. Finally, he noted that performance should be linked to money since it was a motivator (Independence Hall Association, 2013).

As school enrollments grew, especially in urban areas, and graded school structures emerged, public school supervisors felt pressures to implement Taylor's management principles. School leaders began to identify more efficient ways to organize curriculum, structure schools, and teach children. They also considered how best to measure teacher performance. Taylor's scientific management principles ushered in a new era in public education during which expectations for educators to increase their organizational efficiency and raise teacher performance became priorities.

EARLY TEACHER EVALUATION

In response to the business world emphasis on specialization and increased efficiencies, early teacher evaluation focused on desired teacher performance behaviors. It was also supervisor driven. McGreal (1983) labeled this early evaluation approach the Common Law Model. Although no one individual is credited with its development, the Common Law Model became the approach of choice.

The Common Law Model is a top-down teacher evaluation process built on the identification of performance expectations and evaluation procedures. Supervisors identify what they expect teachers to do and rate them on how well they perform. The emphasis is on administrator feedback, not collaborative discussions with teachers.

According to McGreal (1983), Common Law Models have six characteristics.

- High supervisor–low teacher involvement. Under this top-down evaluation approach, administrators tell teachers how well they performed. The role of the teacher is passive participant.
- Observation and evaluation are synonymous. Classroom observation serves as the primary basis for the summative evaluation. Often a teacher's evaluation is based on a single, annual classroom observation plus general evaluator perceptions.
- Nondifferentiation in procedures for tenured and nontenured teachers. Common Law Models treat tenured and nontenured teachers similarly. Both the evaluation criteria and the actual process are usually identical. The primary difference is that nontenured teachers are observed more often than their tenured colleagues.
- High emphasis on summative evaluation. The primary focus of evaluation is the overall performance of teachers, not their professional development.
- Use of standardized criteria. School districts establish local criteria, which are applied to all teaching positions regardless of grade level or teaching assignment. The model is often a one-fit-all approach

for all teachers regardless of teaching assignment or responsibilities.

- Forced comparisons. Since common law approaches include ratings, they are often used to compare, not develop, teachers.

The most popular type of Common Law Model is a checklist of performance expectations. These are usually accompanied by rating scales. Sometimes narrative descriptions of performance are used in place of checklists. However, in all instances, administrators judge teacher performance against specific expectations. Typical examples of checklist descriptors include:

- Follows approved curriculum;
- Exhibits effective classroom management skills;
- Maintains a classroom environment conducive to learning; and
- Follows district and school policies and procedures.

Although the number of school districts that formally evaluated teachers during this time was far less than today, the Common Law Model established a standard for teacher performance and evaluation. It also signaled the beginning of increased expectations for school supervisors to monitor and rate teacher performance. To this day, elements of the Common Law Model can be found in numerous school district teacher evaluation processes.

EMPHASIS ON INSTRUCTIONAL IMPROVEMENT

By the mid-1900s, the focus on teacher evaluation began to evolve beyond general performance standards. Some educators called for a shift in teacher supervision focus toward an emphasis on the teaching skills and the teachers' individual needs. Although initially this shift was more prevalent in educational rhetoric than actual practice, it ushered in a new era in supervision (Marzano, Frontier, & Livingston, 2011).

What helped accelerate the call for more personalized evaluation methods was the "Cold War" of propaganda with the Soviet Union beginning in the 1950s. Initially, this shocked many post–World War II Americans who believed the United States was the premier world leader. Suddenly, Americans watched as Russia emerged as a growing and powerful international competitor.

This conflict played out on numerous political and societal fronts, but initially had little direct impact on public education. As the Soviet Union pursued its political agenda, competition for international leadership supremacy between the countries grew. It ultimately reached a crescendo with the successful launch of Sputnik in 1957 (Garber, 2007).

With Sputnik, the United States had lost the race to space. The Soviet Union had asserted itself prominently on the international stage. This event coupled with declining student performance on the Scholastic Aptitude Test (SAT) and general societal unrest in the 1960s helped drive the perception that current teacher evaluation methods were inadequate.

As this perception grew, so did calls to improve educational performance. Simultaneously, questions were raised about the efficacy of both the nation's public education system and school district leadership. Educators watched as the public suddenly expressed concerns about the quality of the American educational system, especially math and science instruction.

Educators, who had grown accustomed to ongoing and unwavering public support, found themselves facing questions and criticisms about the quality of public education. School administrators quickly discovered that being an efficient manager was no longer sufficient. They faced a public that demanded answers and educational improvements. The status quo was no longer the primary yardstick of success. Instead, the race was on to reclaim the United States' status as a global powerhouse, in which education was a key factor.

Educators responded to this challenge by re-tooling some aspects of the teacher evaluation process. As calls for accountability mounted, the efficacy of the Common Law Model was questioned. Stakeholders pointed out that if it was not producing the desired results, another approach should be considered. One response was the introduction of the Goal Setting Model (McGreal, 1983).

Goal Setting Model

While the Common Law Model was global in focus and targeted general performance expectations, the Goal Setting Model was highly personalized. Its underlying premise was simple. Those supporting a goal setting approach argued that teachers themselves were in the best position to assess their own strengths and weaknesses. They reasoned that allowing teachers to set their own personal goals would lead to improved performance (McGreal, 1983).

As the Goal Setting Model grew in popularity, school districts began to include this approach in their district teacher evaluation processes. To implement the Goal Setting Model, teachers and administrators met annually to formulate individual teacher goals, which were evaluated at the end of the school year during the summative evaluation conference.

Similar to Common Law Model, this approach ultimately proved insufficient as a performance assessment tool. Although it did increase communication between teachers and administrators, it was not useful in rating teacher performance. It did not lead to measureable improvements in teaching and learning. Many of the personal goals were inconsequential and unrelated to effective instruction. Also, often the evaluation process itself lacked rigor. Yet, the goal setting approach found its way into

teacher evaluation plans in school districts across the country. Even today, school district teacher evaluation processes often include a goal setting component.

Product Model

Throughout the 1960s, school administrators experienced a rapid
change in leadership expectations from manager to instructional leader.
Passage of legislation such as the Elementary and Secondary Education
Act (ESEA) of 1965, which required administrators to implement new
programs and services, contributed to the expanded role. Under ESEA,
states that sought federal funding were required to offer programs and
services serving the needs of disadvantaged students. In addition, they
had to provide increased professional development (Beyer & Johnson,
2005). For the first time, school administrators were called upon to take
the lead in implementing sweeping educational change.

As the concept of measuring teacher and/or student performance
gained wider attention with educators, political leaders, and other interested groups, the focus on performance indicators only grew. Spurring
calls for change during the 1960s and 1970s were data showing that student achievement continued to remain flat or had even declined. As a
consequence, the age of measuring student performance with more concrete data was born.

One of the innovations during the 1970s was the introduction of performance objectives. Teachers were asked to identify very specific student learning objectives and either design assessment measures or review
student achievement results on norm-referenced tests to assess student
mastery. These early data-based assessments led to the introduction of a
new teacher evaluation model called the Product Model (McGreal, 1983).

What was most significant about the Product Model was that it expanded national attention on teacher performance evaluation. Up to this
point, teacher evaluation methods were largely targeted at the "what" of
teaching. That is, evaluators made judgments about what teachers did
and what they taught. Under the Product Model, supervisors now became concerned with teaching outcomes. A small number of school districts even began to tie student performance on standardized tests to
teacher and administrative evaluation. Although the early implementation was largely loosely defined, it proved to be the beginning of student
assessment–based teacher evaluation.

Over the next few decades, subsequent federal administrations working with Congress have increased the emphasis on measuring student
achievement through the reauthorized ESEA. In each instance, assessing
student performance only increased. The most recent version in 2001, No
Child Left Behind (NCLB), included mandatory student achievement
performance benchmarks (Beyer & Johnson, 2005). Clearly, the success of

teachers and administrators was inextricably linked to measurable student achievement.

In the wake of ESEA, public education has been hit with waves of educational reform. Each has targeted some aspect of student learning related to teacher performance and administrative leadership. One prominent effort during the 1970s was the Effective Schools Research (ESR).

EFFECTIVE SCHOOLS MOVEMENT

Ronald Edmonds, director of the Center for Urban Studies at Harvard University, undertook research in public schools to identify why disadvantaged students in particular schools out-performed those in other schools even though they had similar demographic profiles (Association for Effective Schools, 2012). His research was foundational in advancing the concept that classroom teachers make a difference. It countered the belief that student socioeconomic status was the major factor related to student achievement.

From this research emerged seven correlates of effective schools. Each was linked in some way to teacher performance or administrative leadership. These correlates included:

- Clear school mission;
- High expectations for success;
- Instructional leadership;
- Frequent monitoring of student progress;
- Opportunities to learn and student on-task time;
- Safe and orderly environment; and
- Home-school relations (Association for Effective Schools, Inc., 1996).

ESR helped advance a national focus on the "what" and "how" of teaching and administrative leadership. Educators across the country turned their attention to identifying specific characteristics of schools that had been shown to be related to increased student achievement. Ultimately, ESR directly influenced administrative leadership and teaching performance. It cemented the shift in a principal's role from operational manager to instructional leader (Nettles & Herrington, 2007).

During this 1980s, the US Department of Education under the direction of the Reagan administration used ESR as the foundation for its National Blue Ribbon Schools Program, a nation-wide school recognition program. This national award program was designed to identify and recognize public and private schools that had shown school improvement and increased student achievement. Recognized schools were judged on how well they met each of the ESR correlates. By honoring ESR exemplary schools, political leaders hoped to encourage all educators and school boards to strive for educational improvement (U.S. Department of Education, 2013).

EFFECTIVE TEACHING MOVEMENT

During this same period, researchers also studied links between classroom instruction and student achievement. Their research further documented the direct impact teachers can have on student learning. At the forefront was Madeline Hunter from the Graduate School of Education at University of California at Los Angeles. As principal of the University Elementary School in the 1960s, she spearheaded a research movement that focused on teaching and learning (Hunter, 1982).

Hunter studied how a particular lesson structure could improve student learning. Her lesson design model identified seven important elements teachers should consider when planning and teaching their lessons (Hunter, 1982). These elements included:

- Providing lesson objectives that let students know what they should understand or be able to do by the end of the lesson;
- Considering input, which she defined as teachers providing students with the knowledge or skills students need to learn;
- Modeling to demonstrate the skill or competency taught;
- Checking for understanding to ensure students have learned the objectives;
- Ensuring opportunities for guided practice so students could apply new learning under teacher supervision;
- Bringing closure to a lesson, which meant reviewing with students what they had learned during the class; and
- Assigning independent practice or opportunities to practice what was learned without teacher guidance.

Hunter and her co-researchers never intended the model to be applied rigidly to all instructional situations. Rather, it was designed as a framework around which teachers should make decisions about components appropriate to their lessons. Nonetheless, in their effort to improve instruction, some administrators embraced it as the answer to instructional improvement. In some schools, administrators required teachers to uniformly implement the lesson design framework in their daily lesson plans. In others, the framework was used as a checklist to determine teacher effectiveness. Other schools even routinely tied the framework to the district teacher evaluation plan (Berg & Clough, 1990).

What is most important about Hunter's lesson design model was not the efficacy of the framework itself. Her long-lasting contribution to teaching, supervision, and teacher evaluation was that she identified connections between what teachers and administrators do and student learning.

Clinical Supervision

As part of the movement to make teaching, learning, and supervision more scientific, the importance of teacher evaluation as an administrative responsibility grew. What emerged in response was the Clinical Supervision Model. Under the clinical supervision process popularized during the 1970s and 1980s, teachers and building administrators focused much more closely on the "what and how" of teaching. Although the model was not new at the time, it grew in popularity as it gained national attention beginning in the mid-1970s. Rather than focusing on meeting district performance standards or measuring student achievement gains, clinical supervision targeted what teachers did in their classrooms.

Principals were asked to step out of their offices and into classrooms to work directly with teachers on instructional issues. Administrators were trained to collect evidence through direct classroom observation focused on specific research-based effective teaching behaviors. There was an increased emphasis on administrators providing teachers with feedback following observations.

Educators across the country began to integrate formative clinical supervision cycles into their existing teacher evaluation systems. The clinical supervision process consisted of a pre-observation conference, lesson observation, and post-observation conference. At the early implementation stage, evaluators conducted pre-observation conferences with teachers targeted at individual class sessions. During the pre-observation conference, the teacher described in detail the lesson to be observed. Often the focus of the pre-conference included one or more of Hunter's lesson design components. Together the administrator and the teacher agreed on the parameters and focus of the classroom observation. However, under the clinical supervision model, the emphasis was solely on teacher behaviors with little or no regard for student outcomes.

After observing the lesson, teachers and administrators met to discuss the observation. On a conceptual level, administrators were expected to work with classroom teachers through this process to improve their teaching performance. In this role, administrators were expected to provide teachers with constructive feedback based on effective teaching behaviors. Teachers were also encouraged to offer their perspectives. An expected outcome of this process was the overall improvement of instruction through feedback and evaluation.

Educational researchers during the clinical supervision period such as Madeline Hunter, M. D. Gall, and Keith Acheson became household names. Administrators drew from their work, as well as that of others, important information that they used to develop local clinical observation processes. This emphasis on instructional improvement helped establish the standard for principals as instructional leaders. Through the clinical supervision process, they were expected to discuss classroom instruction with teachers and offer suggestions for improvement and professional growth.

The original clinical supervision process, however, retained a summative flavor. Although teachers were brought into the supervision and evaluation processes more as colleagues than subordinates, administrators were still expected to tell teachers how they were performing. One positive outcome of the clinical supervision movement was that it increased the amount of time that administrators spent in classrooms. It also signaled a shift of perceived administrative priorities. No longer was it acceptable for administrators to be simply good managers. They were now expected to lead instructional improvement.

As with prior supervision reforms, clinical supervision had an important impact on the continued improvement of supervision and teacher evaluation practices. Today, clinical supervision components remain integral elements of most school district teacher evaluation plans. Yet, clinical supervision did not satisfy stakeholder expectations for increased student achievement. Growing concerns about the quality of public education continued to mount.

A NATION AT RISK

As the focus on improved teaching and learning expanded in the aftermath of Sputnik, another major attack on education was symbolized by the publication of *A Nation at Risk* (1983). This report contributed to a growing chorus of public education criticism. The report famously noted that the decline in public education was a more serious threat to Americans than any war the nation ever faced.

In its report, the National Commission on Excellence in Education (1983) described multiple "Indicators of Risk," which were examples of how public schools had failed. The report called upon Americans to take immediate action or face dire consequences that would undermine the economic foundation of our country.

One statement in the report best summarizes the Commission's findings.

> Each generation of Americans has outstripped its parents in education, in literacy, and in economics. For the first time in the history of our country, the educational skills of one generation will not surpass, will not equal, will not even approach, those of their parents. (National Commission on Excellence in Education, 1983)

Soon national leaders from any number of professions, even education, began to demand more concrete evidence of student achievement gains. Just developing new curricula, expanding professional development, utilizing evolving teacher evaluation methods, or discussing what teachers and students did were insufficient. The public insisted on measurable results. As a consequence, the metric of choice that grew in popularity was the standardized achievement test.

WAVES OF EDUCATIONAL REFORM

During the last half of the 1980s, state legislatures became increasingly impatient with the pace of local reforms. As a result, they began to assert themselves more directly into the reform process through the passage of sweeping legislation. In Illinois, for example, the state legislature with the support of the governor passed broad-based legislation requiring K–12 public schools to implement a variety of reform measures designed to hold educators more accountable.

Some of the key Illinois provisions included:

- Mandatory teacher evaluation requirements that included classroom observation and overall summative evaluation of teacher performance;
- A system of common state-wide academic assessments at benchmark grade levels;
- Required administrative training on state-mandated teacher evaluation guidelines; and
- State school report cards, which provided the public with key school district student assessment data.

As these state-specific initiatives swept the country, teacher evaluation processes continued to evolve. In particular, educators sought to improve clinical supervision by increasing the emphasis on teacher reflection over supervisory feedback.

EMPHASIS ON TEACHER REFLECTION

During the 1990s, the clinical supervision approach to teacher evaluation was modified to provide an increased emphasis on teacher reflection. Rather than stressing administrative feedback following observations, reformers encouraged more formative approaches. Administrators assumed a more collegial role in the overall process. Teachers were encouraged to be self-reflective. Under the reflective model, teachers were expected to think more deeply about what they did and why they did it. The rationale for this refinement was that encouraging teachers to become more metacognitive about their craft would lead to more effective instruction and subsequently increased student achievement.

Elements of both the clinical and reflective approaches are still prevalent in school districts today. However, pressure to effectively measure and improve student achievement has only continued to increase. Principals, assistant principals, department chairs, and other evaluators today feel more pressure than ever to produce results. Political and community leaders continue to demand that administrators hold teachers to high standards of accountability.

MEASURING STUDENT ACHIEVEMENT

By the mid-1990s, the national pattern of reform was also becoming more defined. More than ever, administrators were expected to publicly demonstrate school improvement and student achievement growth. However, what also emerged was increased debate about how best to define and measure student achievement.

For the general public, the answer was simple—achievement test results. Others, primarily educators, argued that achievement test results were too narrowly focused to be a true indicator of overall student achievement. They also pointed to research showing that educators had little control over factors such as the socioeconomic level of families or the life experiences of children. These, they pointed out, directly affect student performance on standardized achievement assessments.

As this debate continued into the 2000s, public sentiment increasingly supported the use of achievement test scores as the metric of choice. Under President George W. Bush and with the bipartisan support of key Democratic party leaders, the nation's public schools were required for the first time in history to demonstrate graduated student achievement proficiency through NCLB. Schools that failed to meet increasing target achievement levels in reading and mathematics were subject to sanctions. This change propelled the national discussion on how best to improve student achievement.

STANDARDS MOVEMENT

As the push for data-driven assessments grew, so too did calls for national standards. In 2010, the National Governors Association (NGA) and Council of Chief State School Officers (CCSSO) (2010) released the Common Core Standards in Mathematics and English/Language Arts. The goal of the commission was to encourage states to replace their own standards by adopting a common set of national standards by 2015. To date, most states have adopted these standards and are working together to develop standardized assessments aligned with the Common Core

Standards. Ultimately, the hope is that a common national assessment will emerge.

The national standards movement has also led to changes in teacher supervision and evaluation. As teacher evaluation has become more directly linked with summative performance assessment, the effectiveness of reflective clinical supervision to improve teacher performance has come under increased scrutiny. Researchers such as Danielson (2012) have argued that:

- Teacher observations and the evaluation process must be grounded in research-based and validated practices;
- Clear performance levels must be defined and understood by all;
- Observers must have the skills to conduct fair and reliable teacher observations;
- Evidence collection must be thorough, consistent, and properly interpreted against defined performance levels regardless of who conducts the observation; and
- Professional conversations with teachers should be integral to any process.

The history of teacher supervision and evaluation in the United States is long and complex. Over centuries, it has grown in sophistication as researchers have honed in on what is known about how students learn, teachers teach, and administrators supervise. Although great progress has been made, much more is yet to come. By understanding the history of teacher supervision and evaluation, today's researchers and evaluators are better positioned to continue to define and improve teaching and student learning.

IMPLICATIONS FOR TODAY'S ADMINISTRATORS

Administrators today are expected to devote a substantial portion of their time to instructional issues with a primary focus on improving student learning. The days of the former coach turned principal managing the day-to-day operations of the school and leaving what went on in the classroom to teachers have all but vanished.

At the same time, much more is known about what teachers and administrators can do to increase student achievement. Researchers such as Tucker and Stronge (2005), Danielson (2007), Hattie (2009), and Darling-Hammond (2010) have documented the impact that both effective and ineffective teachers have on student achievement. They have also identified how administrators can provide effective leadership to improve teaching and learning.

To meet these increased expectations, administrators must have a much more thorough understanding of curriculum, instruction, and data analysis than ever before if they are to be effective leaders. They must understand the latest research and best practices in hiring, supervising, and evaluating teachers if they are to employ and develop faculty members who can truly make a difference in student achievement.

Over the next few years, administrators will face more and more pressure from parents, boards of education, political leaders, and a host of others with an interest in public education to ensure teaching excellence. This will include holding teachers much more accountable for their performance including documenting teacher effectiveness and student learning. At the same time, the same public will raise the bar on administrative performance.

POINTS TO REMEMBER

Over the past 400 years, the role of school administrators has expanded exponentially. Administrators today cannot succeed by simply managing their schools well. They must be true instructional leaders who understand how to improve schools, ensure high levels of teacher performance, and improve student achievement. At the same time, they must have the personal skills to work effectively with a multitude of stakeholders.

To accomplish this, school administrators must be proactive leaders who are up-to-date in the field. They must have a thorough understanding of the latest research in teaching, supervision, and evaluation related to improving schools and boosting student achievement. They must recognize that these expectations will only grow. Finally, they must demonstrate the initiative and fortitude to enhance their leadership practices.

TWO

Recruiting and Selecting Outstanding Teachers

One of the most important decisions you make as an administrator is the selection of personnel, especially teachers. How thoughtfully and thoroughly you approach this process will have a tremendous impact on the quality of teachers you hire. It will also directly affect the number and types of problems you will encounter on a daily basis.

CHALLENGES IN TEACHER SELECTION

Principals are very busy people. Rarely do they find themselves with extra time on their hands. More often than not, they feel pressure from their superintendents, board members, staff, and parents to accomplish more than can be done in a day. This pressure is particularly acute during the last half of the school year, a critical time period for hiring faculty members.

As an administrator, you, too, will experience the crunch of the end of the school year, which will impact your hiring effectiveness. However, if you learn to recognize and subsequently adjust to these inevitable challenges, you can minimize their impact. This will increase the time you have to focus on teacher selection.

Challenge 1: Permitting day-to-day issues to interfere with the selection process. If you wait until you feel you have more time for teacher selection, it will be at least mid-June before you start the process. This will not allow you to be thoughtful and thorough. At the same time, you may find a shallower candidate pool. By placing a high priority on hiring as early as possible, you will be more efficient. Simultaneously, you will reduce many of the pressures of last-minute hiring on yourself and others.

To overcome these challenges, consider the following strategies:

- Meet with your superintendent and/or other central office administrators in November or December to discuss the district hiring process. It is important to work collaboratively with them to ensure you are all on the "same page." This will help you avoid miscommunication and other problems while freeing more time for hiring. By doing so, you will also send the message that hiring is one of your top priorities.
- Define a thorough and efficient school-level candidate selection process that works for you. Invite others you intend to involve to contribute their suggestions. They may offer useful ideas that you may not have considered. By doing so, you build support for the process while ensuring that they understand their roles and responsibilities.
- Consider prescheduling potential interview dates in January extending through May. At first, this may seem too early. However, you will appreciate this preplanning later. Make sure you consult with other administrators who will participate. This simple organization strategy will improve your hiring efficiency and help you avoid the inevitable email or phone tag frustrations associated with on-the-spot scheduling.
- Avoid the temptation to schedule other activities on pre-set interview days. It is easy to fill these dates with other responsibilities. Try to hold them open until you know they will not be needed.
- Consider conducting preliminary screening interviews during winter break. Sometimes you know you need to fill a particular position. Other times you want to be prepared for potential or unexpected last-minute openings. Winter break is an excellent time to devote to application review and initial screening. Since most staff members are off for an extended period of time, you can make good use of this quiet time.

Challenge 2: Letting others dictate the selection process. Successful administrators are never laissez-faire leaders. Unfortunately, some principals operate under the mistaken assumption that if they delegate the selection process to teachers, they will increase staff member support. These principals either fail to define the process clearly or turn over the decision-making responsibility almost entirely to teachers. In the end, this will actually weaken a principal's position. In addition, it will most likely lead to the selection of teachers who are status quo–oriented.

The most successful administrators, on the other hand, are willing to take charge. They clarify the selection process steps. They also clearly define each participant's role in the process. In short, they exert strong leadership.

If you are new to your position, though, proceed slowly. You need to respect past practice. If you are too assertive and make too many changes too quickly, you can hurt your credibility.

As the school's leader, you should be the one who initiates the process. This means defining the steps, establishing the timeline, and clarifying who participates as well as their responsibilities. By taking such proactive leadership, you strengthen your position as the school leader and minimize opportunities for others to steer the selection.

Challenge 3: Getting bogged down during the selection process. Although it is important to ensure that your teacher selection process is comprehensive, you should avoid becoming its captive. Even though you may have established very definitive selection process steps, you must remain flexible. Rather than rigidly implementing each procedural step no matter what, you should use your best judgment at key junctures. For example, if you have to move up a screening interview to accommodate a particular candidate, do so. If a candidate has a pending offer, look for a way to alter your process to ensure that you can give the person full consideration. Administrators who are too dogmatic can undermine their success with their inflexibility.

Challenge 4: Honoring the process. While it is important to maintain flexibility, you must also avoid "falling in love" with candidates without adequate information. Before speeding through the selection, make sure you know who you are hiring. You may need to temper your intuition by not reacting too quickly. A common mistake is quickly determining that candidates are a good fit then rushing the process. If you do, you may miss signs that indicate incompatibility.

TEACHER SELECTION

Once you have considered these roadblocks, you are ready to begin the hiring process. The first step is recruitment. Remember that your top priority during the recruitment phase is to maximize your candidate pool. In addition, you want to ensure that you reach as many highly qualified and diverse candidates as possible. It is not sufficient to have a large candidate pool if it only consists of marginally prepared individuals who do not reflect your school district's diversity.

Building a Strong Applicant Pool

The only candidates you can consider for a position are those who actually apply. Although this sounds rather simplistic, too many administrators fail to place a high enough priority on recruiting. Rather, they rely primarily on candidates who happen to apply. More often than not, these tend to be individuals who are currently employed in the school as teacher assistants or substitute teachers or have some other connection to the district.

If you employ this approach, your candidate pool will likely be weak. If you do identify strong candidates, it will be more by coincidence than from good planning. As a consequence, you will find yourself selecting from an average to even weak pool if you rely solely on unsolicited candidates.

A better approach is to "leave no stone unturned" in your quest for candidates. The strongest candidates tend to be available earlier rather than later in the process. As a result, you must be an aggressive recruiter. You cannot rely exclusively on your central office administrators or known candidates for your pool.

You must recognize that you have to go beyond the simple tried and true recruitment strategies of the past. Candidates today no longer simply check university placement bulletins for vacancies. In fact, unlike even just a few years ago, they no longer "blanket the market area" with hardcopies of their resumes and cover letters. If you are to develop a strong applicant pool, you need to adjust your recruitment to reflect current trends. Here are several strategies to consider.

Strategy 1: Think technology. Young adults have grown up with technology. If they want information, they pull out their smart phones and search for it. Most have never heard the term credential file or even considered contacting their university for assistance finding teaching positions. To be a successful recruiter, you must be in the electronic recruitment market.

To do so, begin by posting your vacancies in those places applicants are likely to find them electronically. These include:

- Listing vacancies prominently on your district website. Make sure your website is designed for candidate convenience. The more visible you make your vacancies, the better. With a simple click of the mouse, someone should be able to access any opening.
- Asking your teachers to email an announcement of a specific vacancy to members of professional groups to which they belong. This approach can be especially effective for specialized openings such as a Spanish teaching vacancy.
- Investing in online application software that meets your needs. Candidates are more likely to complete an online application if you provide them with a quick link to a simple application.
- Avoiding the temptation to require applicants to provide unnecessary and extensive information on their applications. This can discourage them from applying. Rather, ask yourself what is the minimum information you need. Some school districts require applicants to respond to extensive philosophical questions, which are of

minimal use. Consider for a moment whether you would be more likely to apply to a district if you had to complete a complicated application.

- Investigating opportunities to connect with university administrators who will publicize your vacancies through their listservs or email blasts.
- Identifying web-based recruiting sources in your area. Assemble a comprehensive list of web-based vacancy listings in your market area. It is quite common for professional organizations, state boards of education, and county regional offices of education to maintain listings of teacher vacancies. If you regularly advertise on these sites, you can reach thousands of candidates very efficiently and cost effectively.
- Being willing to spend funds to advertise for specialized positions such as occupational therapists and Mandarin Chinese teachers. This is often more affordable than you think, especially if you target industry-specific journals or professional organizations.

Strategy 2: Promote your school district. In what type of school district would you rather be employed? Would it be one with the best reputation or one associated with problems? Applicants, especially those in high demand areas, will be more inclined to apply to school districts with reputations for excellence.

An effective way to determine how applicants may view your school district is to research it yourself on the Internet. Through this approach, you will be directed to news stories and other information they see when conducting their research.

You cannot control everything written or posted online about your school district. However, you can ensure that positive information, including district accomplishments, is highlighted to the public. Here are several ways to approach this.

- When you go online, evaluate how well your district programs, services, and accomplishments are promoted. Take advantage of every opportunity you have to make positive district and school information available on the Web. Emphasize aspects of your district that make it a desirable place to work and learn.
- Ramp up your online publications on your website or other available electronic sources. Rather than relying primarily on hardcopy media, expand you online presence.
- Encourage staff to serve the community and their professional organizations. Their successes, which reflect well on your district, will likely make their way to the Web.
- Be sure that website content is up-to-date. Candidates notice if information is dated.

Strategy 3: Look for opportunities to recruit collaboratively through electronic sources.   In addition to school district–driven recruiting, consider teaming with other school districts. If you have an ongoing working relationship with other school districts, suggest that you promote each other's openings. For example, you might maintain a consortium webpage or agree on a common application. On this site, you could include a vacancy listing service with weblinks to individual school districts and their vacancies. Before long, you will find that candidates bookmark this page. They will see it as a convenient way to find multiple district vacancies.

Strategy 4: Ramp up your networking.   Never underestimate the value of personal contact. You never know when or where you might meet an ideal candidate or connect with someone who will make a referral. To expand your candidate pool, let administrators, teachers, support staff, and others know that you are interested in their recommendations. This approach does not commit you to hiring someone. However, it does broaden your recruiting efforts.

Similarly, adopt a broad meet-and-greet philosophy. Although your time or that of other administrators might be tight, place a priority on making yourself available for casual conversations with anyone offering a referral. Better yet, offer to meet informally with anyone referred. The few minutes you spend will encourage them to submit an application.

Strategy 5: Ensure that your district or school is represented at job fairs.   Another way to broaden your recruiting is to participate in local and regional job fairs. These will allow you to meet potential teachers who may be unfamiliar with your school district or who would otherwise never apply. Many universities, consortiums of universities, professional organizations, or groups of school districts sponsor job fairs.

Job fairs can be overwhelming for both candidates and employers. However, with some good planning, you can turn them into a productive recruiting tool. Here are guidelines you could use to make job fair recruiting more efficient and effective.

- Select a district or school team to conduct the interviews.
- Limit interviews to five minutes or less.
- Create a positive public relations information sheet about your school and district to distribute and/or display on an information board.
- Train team members on what to ask. Include questions about qualifications and personal qualities. Prepare them to make snap judgments based on district-identified criteria.
- Do not be too discriminating. Try to identify a larger rather than smaller pool of potential "yes" candidates. They can be screened later to narrow the applicant pool.

- Have written information available for candidates on how to complete the application process. You may even have a computer available for them to apply onsite.
- Schedule a meeting with interview team members as soon as possible after they return from the job fair. During this session, target the most viable candidates for further consideration.
- Make sure you identify promising candidates even in areas where you presently do not have a vacancy. You never know when someone may submit a resignation (Kersten, 2010).

Job fairs can be an effective recruiting approach if used well.

Minority Recruiting

One mistake administrators make is assuming that minority candidates will seek out their districts. If you hope to attract a more diverse candidate pool, you must be a more systematic recruiter. To accomplish this, consider the following approaches.

- Network with college of education faculty members at schools with diverse student bodies. By volunteering to speak to education classes or inviting faculty members to visit or assist you in your district and school, you can establish personalized, ongoing communication.
- Identify minority educators who can help you find candidates.
- Think like the National Football League, which requires all teams to interview a minority candidate for every coaching position. If at all possible, try to identify some minority candidates for every vacancy.
- Seek out opportunities to recruit at the universities with significant minority student populations.
- Participate in job fairs that include universities with substantial diverse student enrollments.
- Ensure that any district communication tools, either hardcopy or online, reflect a commitment to diversity.

By marketing your vacancies directly to diverse candidates, you will increase your minority candidate pool.

Focusing Your Applicant Screening

If you have been a successful recruiter, you will have generated hundreds or perhaps thousands of applicants. Depending upon your district's use of technology, you will either have an extensive file of hardcopy or electronic applications to consider. Your first challenge is to identify those to move to the interview stage.

Here are approaches that will help you make your process more efficient.

- Ensure that the system you use to store applications is organized logically. Consider the various vacancy categories you will need. Structure your application processing system to match.
- Take advantage of online application process routing capabilities. Most offer an instant notification feature, which you can set to send you an email whenever an application is received for a specific position. This service is very useful for openings that will likely field shallow pools of candidates.
- Work with your administrative staff to identify the "first cut" criteria. Once you agree on criteria, you can begin to sort candidates in "Yes" and "No" categories. This will substantially reduce the number of applications you will need to review when you begin to fill vacancies.
- Establish procedures to implement your screening process on a continuous basis. How this is accomplished varies from district to district. However, if done daily, you will find application screening less overwhelming.
- Use sorting procedures built into online application software. Application software often permits screeners to rate candidates. When it is time for interviews, you can select only those with specific ratings. Many also have electronic folders or pipelines to help organize applications as you sort them.
- Access applicant filtering procedures common to electronic applications. You can sort applications by such criteria as experience, certification, grade point average, level of education, and more. Another common feature allows you to set specific applicant criteria. Candidates who met the criteria have their applications sent to a specific folder.
- Purchase a candidate screener. Companies that provide teacher selection process systems often sell a simple teacher assessment/ screener, which could be useful as an initial candidate screener.
- Work with key district personnel to further refine selection criteria before you are screening applicants. If all administrators thoroughly understand the criteria, they can work as a team to narrow the candidate pool to the most qualified. By spreading the screening task among multiple administrators, you can accomplish more in less time.
- Do not get "hung up" on experience. Teachers with three to five years of experience typically adapt best to new school cultures. In general, it is better to hire a new or less experienced teacher who is more adaptable than a very experienced person who may be too rigid.

Application screening can be time consuming and overwhelming especially with so many demands facing you. However, by starting early and approaching it systematically, you can increase your efficiency.

Ensuring a Comprehensive Interview Process

In addition to building an extensive applicant pool, be certain to design a comprehensive interview process that reflects the culture and complexity of your school district. This means employing sufficient interview layers to increase your chances of selecting the best teacher.

Some applicants have the personal skills to connect with almost anyone. The question is whether they have the complete package. Also, everyone has his or her own strengths and weaknesses. Therefore, you want to make sure you have done your homework. You do not want to be surprised about any candidates after they are hired.

To select the best teacher, you must gather as much information about each candidate as possible as you work through all stages of the teacher selection process. To do so, you want to observe them in multiple settings. Also, you should see a candidate during as many steps of the process as possible. Your goal is to get to know each person as well as you can.

As you begin the interview process, it is useful to conceptualize it as a large funnel. Initially, you interview as many applicants as possible. As you move through a series of interviews and other selection process steps, you continually narrow your candidate pool. At the widest part of the funnel, you should emphasize quantity. The most successful administrators recognize that screening too tightly too early may inadvertently eliminate some very viable candidates.

Screening Interviews

The first step in a comprehensive interview process is the screening interview. At this stage, you make the critical decision about who will move forward in the process. Poor judgments or too narrow a focus at this juncture may translate into an unsatisfactory interview pool.

One of the challenges you will face will be determining the criteria to effectively sort through those candidates invited for screening interviews. Too often, administrators rely on their "gut" reactions. When asked why they chose one candidate over another, their response is, "I liked the candidate more." Do not be mesmerized by big personality candidates whose only talent is that they have exceptionally adept social skills.

As you begin the interview process, remember that hiring is not synonymous with liking. It is, of course, important to feel comfortable with anyone you hire. However, this should not be the overriding criterion.

Depending on the size of your school district, screening interviews can be conducted by district personnel, building administrators, and/or teams of administrators. As you plan for these interviews, be sure that you understand current district practice. If you want to deviate from past practice, discuss your ideas with district administrators. Otherwise, you run the risk of being perceived as an independent contractor rather than a team player.

Ideally, screening interviews should be limited to fifteen to twenty minutes. You have probably participated in interviews where within two or three minutes you knew whether you were interested in a particular candidate. If the interviews were scheduled for thirty minutes or even longer, you probably felt as if you were wasting valuable time. You were!

The purpose of a screening interview is to answer the question, "Is this someone I could potentially see teaching in our school district?" It is not intended to be an in-depth interview. If you schedule longer screening interviews, you will find that you are meeting fewer applicants than you should.

During screening interviews, focus on the candidate's:

- Personal background;
- Professional experiences to date; and
- Interpersonal skills.

This will give you enough information to make a reasonably informed decision.

Also, consider how many questions you can logically ask in such a brief interview. Otherwise, if you have more than one screening interviewer, some may become frustrated if they do not get to ask all their questions. "Round robin" interviewing during which each committee member asks a single question as you move around the table can contribute to this problem. It can also make the interview process feel awkward or choppy. Another approach is to identify one or two individuals to ask all questions. Realistically, in a fifteen-minute interview, you can ask no more than four to six questions.

Think of the screening interview process as a "soft cut." Ask yourself if you are interested enough to invite the candidate back for a longer interview. Make a quick "yes" or "no" decision without being overly judgmental. These interviews allow you to efficiently cull those who are clear misfits.

Finally, here are four points to remember.

- Begin each screening interview by telling candidates that the interview will be brief. Otherwise, interviewees may interpret a short interview as a lack of interest.

- Be courteous by staying on schedule. This can be very difficult for some candidates and require you to politely redirect the over talker.
- Let candidates know that you will not have time to answer candidate questions. This is the most common reason administrators fall behind schedule. Preempt this by informing candidates upfront about the overall process. Let them know that they will be given a chance to ask questions during future stages of the process.
- Follow up quickly with candidates who are eliminated from further consideration. This common courtesy will help ease their anxiety. It will also show others that you are thoughtful and efficient.

Second Level Interviews

In most instances, second interviews, which are usually thirty to forty-five minutes, are an essential step in a comprehensive selection process. They allow you to probe candidates to determine whether they are up-to-date in the field. Just as important, they give you another opportunity to assess which candidates are the best matches for the school and the specific position. Although there is no ideal minimum or maximum number of candidates, a slightly larger rather than smaller number is suggested.

As you plan for these interviews, begin by determining who should participate. It is important to include at least one other administrator. These can be central office administrators, principals, assistant principals, deans, or coordinators. By adding others to the process, you will gather multiple valuable perspectives about each candidate.

It is also important to understand the phenomenon of unequal perspectives. Have you ever worked with certain administrators who time and again seem to select better teachers? Some administrators are more skilled than others at recognizing talent. Their judgments of candidates should carry the most weight in your assessment. If you can, make a point of inviting district administrators with a reputation for hiring well to assist you.

During the screening interviews, you focused on whether each applicant was a general fit for the position. During second level interviews, you should hone in on specifics. This means identifying exactly what traits, knowledge, and skills you are looking for in the successful candidate.

Here are several areas, some of which you might target during these interviews.

- Professional motivation
- Interpersonal skills
- Ability to communicate
- Eye contact

- Effective listening skills
- Appropriate sense of humor
- Knowledge of Common Core Standards
- Openness to coaching
- Common sense and judgment
- Decision-making/problem-solving skills
- Content area knowledge
- Background in effective teaching research
- Knowledge of effective instructional methodology
- Ability and commitment to relationship-building

Too often, administrators "shoot from the hip." They arrive for interviews just in time to begin. Since they are unprepared, they tend to ask generic questions such as: "Tell me about yourself." Others fall into the trap of cliché questions such as: "What are middle school students like?" Another is: "How important is it for teachers to like kids?" Ask yourself if someone's answers to these questions help you learn anything useful.

To make these interviews most productive takes preplanning. By strategizing with key members of the interview team, you can avoid meaningless, time-filler questions. Think through what knowledge and skills you expect candidates to have. If possible, ask others, who will interview with you, to help create the pool of interview questions.

The best interview questions are those that require candidates to describe what they have accomplished and/or explain what they believe. In addition, situational-based questions linked to the specific position will tell you a great deal about what candidates know. They will also provide insights into how candidates might respond in the classroom.

Here are some samples of effective interview questions.

- Describe a personal experience that had an impact on your teaching.
- How would you facilitate communication between home and school?
- What would your worst critic say about you?
- Describe a typical class period.
- What instructional strategies have you found most effective?
- Describe a lesson that was particularly successful and walk me through each stage from planning to delivery.
- Explain what a strong, balanced literacy program would look like in your classroom.
- What research-based teaching strategies have you used?
- What specific strategies would you use to assist students who are struggling in reading and mathematics?
- What do you do when you see a student is not learning?
- What do you do to help students who are continually failing to complete homework?

- Describe the toughest discipline problem you ever encountered and how you handled it.
- If you were having classroom management problems, when would you ask for help, and to whom would you direct your request?
- Describe the best lesson you ever taught and explain why it was great.
- Describe a challenge you encountered during student teaching. What did you learn from it?
- If you were doing something for your students that you knew was right and your principal told you to stop, what would you do?
- Describe a lesson that did not go particularly well. Explain how you used what you learned to improve your teaching.

In today's classrooms, technology is ever prevalent. From interactive whiteboards to tablets and laptops, teachers need to be comfortable using technology as an instructional tool. Our newest teachers typically come with basic technology skills. They use email, the Internet, and apps seamlessly. However, personal technology skills do not necessarily equate to instructional skill. It is important, therefore, to probe applicants on how they integrate technology into their lessons. During the interview process, you should ask key questions that will tell you just how technology savvy candidates are. You also want to see if they know how to use technology effectively as a tool to enhance learning.

Here are several sample technology-based interview questions, which you will find useful.

- Describe a unit or lesson that involved student use of technology. Explain how you believe the technology enhanced learning.
- When you are planning lessons, you have many instructional methodology options available to you. For example, you could have students make a poster or a presentation to demonstrate their knowledge. Or you could require the use of technology. How do you decide when to require them to use technology rather than a more traditional approach?
- With all the technology options available today, how do you decide what type of technology to use with a particular lesson?
- Describe a unit or lesson for which you decided not to use technology. Why did you determine that it was better to not use technology?
- Tell me something you learned during this past year in the area of technology. How did you decide whether or not it would be useful for instruction?
- How do you use technology in your personal life?

In addition to interview questions driven by the interviewer, you can also learn a great deal about candidates by encouraging them to ask questions. What they ask and how they ask it can provide valuable insights into their priorities and values.

After concluding second round interviews, your next step is to identify those to move forward in the process. Key to candidate assessment is remaining as objective as possible. Avoid personality-based decisions. Even if you feel very positive about certain individuals, do not make them finalists unless you are convinced that they have the knowledge and skills you are looking for. This means ensuring a match between the candidate and the important traits, knowledge, and skills you identified earlier.

By implementing a well-planned, systematic second level interview process, you will learn more about each candidate as well as confirm your perspectives to date. This information will help you target specific individuals and provide foci for reference checking.

Reference Checking

After you have completed second level interviews, now is the time to conduct reference checks on those who you are inviting for final interviews. Unfortunately, some administrators ignore this important step or treat reference checking as a mere formality. This can be a crucial mistake. If done well, reference checks can either confirm or bring into question the efficacy of candidates.

To appreciate this point, consider these scenarios. Have you ever had a poor performing teacher resign to take a position with another school district without ever having received a reference call? Were you ever surprised when an administrator checking a reference never asked you anything specific about the person? This happens all the time.

As an administrator, you must ensure that you have done your due diligence. Consider for a moment the reactions you would receive from your community if you hired someone who had a history of student abuse without ever having checked references. Reference checking is not an ironclad guarantee that you know all you need to about candidates. However, it does demonstrate due diligence and can often change your perception about a candidate.

One way to enhance your reference checking is to work with your administrative team to identify the questions each will ask during any reference check. Here are some you may want to consider.

- How long have you known this person?
- Did you supervise and/or evaluate him/her?
- If you knew what you do now, would you re-hire this person?
- Why do you think that this person wants to leave?

- If you ranked this person's performance against others in your school with 1 as highest, what rank would you assign him/her and why?
- Does this candidate "play well" with others?
- Everyone has strengths and areas for growth. What are this person's?
- How would you rate the growth capacity of this person and why?
- Did you have an opening for which this person was qualified? Was the person offered the position?
- Did you release or fail to re-hire this person?

In addition to asking probing reference check questions, good hiring practice requires a reference checking paper trail. Too often, reference checking is simply verbal. A better approach to document your reference checking is to design a single form on which anyone checking references records the following information.

- Name of the candidate
- Name and position of reference
- Date
- Brief written summary of discussion
- Name of administrator conducting the reference check

To be thorough, require that these forms be placed in the confidential section of personnel files of those employed. Should a future problem occur, you will be able to produce documented evidence to support your initial decision.

Some administrators check references by email or automated survey. Be cautious using such an approach. It is easy to make someone sound particularly good via email or a survey. Also, supervisors may be reluctant to provide much specific information. A personal contact offers you the best opportunity for an accurate assessment. Phone reference checks can be more revealing because references tend to be more forthcoming. You can also tell more from the voice tone or inflection.

Most administrators who conduct formal reference checks contact individuals suggested by applicants as well as current and past supervisors. You should require applicants to provide at least two from supervisors including their current one. When a candidate does not include their present supervisor or at least give a satisfactory reason, you should consider this a red flag.

One way to improve your reference checking is to make informal reference checks. This means using as many sources as you have available to find out as much as you can about any viable candidate. Through your career, you have developed an extensive network of professional and personal contacts. When you are considering a person, do not hesitate to tap these network connections. You can ask a person's reference if they can identify another person who would be able to speak about the candidate. These informal, off the record conversations can provide important perspectives on candidates.

It is also good practice to check out candidates' social network sites. You should also Google their names. Do not rely exclusively on formal reference checks. Make informal reference checking a regular part of your teacher selection process.

Support Staff Involvement

Administrators sometimes forget that they have another important source of applicant assessment available in their support staff. As you begin the selection process, prepare your support staff, including receptionists and secretaries, to offer their opinions on applicants after they interact with them. They typically arrange interviews, answer applicant questions, and greet them as they arrive for interviews. How candidates treat staff members should be a factor in your assessment of them.

Final Interview

By the time you have narrowed your applicant pool to the final two to four candidates for a position, you usually have a good sense of each person's strengths and weaknesses. However, you have probably not assessed their written communication skills. During the final interview, build in a simple writing assessment activity. This will allow you to judge their skills.

When finalists are scheduled, inform them that they will be asked to provide a brief writing sample. Let them know that you will provide everything necessary and that no preparation is required. Although this may create some anxiety for candidates, it is an effective way for you to assess their basic writing skills.

For the task, identify a grade level appropriate topic about which teachers would prepare a written document for parents. For example, elementary teachers often email or send home a letter to parents following the first day of class to introduce themselves and provide information that sets the tone for the year.

For the writing sample, create a prompt that provides only the most basic information needed. Also, define the amount of time they have to complete it. Finally, provide them with a computer and printer on which to compose their letter. This impromptu writing exercise will tell you a great deal about their writing and even technology skills.

After they complete the written assignment, they are ready for their interview. Similar to prior interviews, it is useful to invite others to participate. You should consider including other building or district administrators. However, you may also want to involve teachers. If you are new to the school, investigate if and how they have been included in the past.

If you do invite teachers, decide who should attend (grade level colleagues, other content area teachers, teacher leaders, etc.). Also, make sure that you either integrate them into the interview team or sit with them during any teacher-only interview. Of course, it is very important to make sure that the teachers understand that their role in the process is advisory. This means establishing clear expectations for team members. Let them know the format for the process and how you will gather their feedback at the end.

Once these interviews are completed, you should have gathered enough information to narrow your choice to one or two preferred candidates. Yet, to be thorough, one additional step remains—demonstration teaching.

Demonstration Teaching

Have you ever hired a teacher who could "talk a good game" but not perform? Most administrators have. Some individuals are superb interviewers. They breeze through each interview. Everyone who meets them is impressed with how they present themselves.

A mistake some administrators can make is offering someone a position prior to observing them teach. By observing your final candidate(s) in front of children, you will learn whether they possess basic teaching ability. You will also discover whether they naturally relate well with students.

When using a demonstration lesson, do not expect teaching perfection. Instead, recognize that no matter how well it is structured, the lesson will appear somewhat artificial. However, during the demo lesson, you can observe their basic teaching style and see how they might react in supervisory situations.

A demonstration teaching lesson consists of four parts:

- Lesson preparation
- Pre-observation conferencing
- Observation
- Post-observation conferencing

It is best to conduct the demo lesson in the school and at the grade level of the vacancy. By expecting any candidates to teach in your school, rather than their own or where they presently student teach or teach, you eliminate many variables. If it is summer, you may have to use a summer school class not directly related to the opening. The only time to forego this step is when you have no option.

Lesson Preparation

Up to this point in the process, all candidate information has been by document or conversation. You have yet to observe any applicant working directly with students. During the demonstration lesson, you will have the opportunity to observe them put their words into actions.

After establishing a date and time with the candidate for the demonstration lesson, have him or her meet with the classroom teacher to prepare for the observation. It is preferable to provide two options. One is to allow the candidate to work with the regular classroom teacher to extend the current unit of study. Under this approach, the demonstration lesson is a natural extension of instruction. Another is to allow the person to select a lesson of choice. In either instance, what is chosen, and how it is delivered will be instructive. Almost as important will be how the prospective teacher works with the regular classroom teacher.

Demonstration lessons can be shorter than a traditional classroom period. To be most efficient, consider requiring candidates to teach a twenty-minute "mini-lesson." You can learn what you need to in this period of time. You will also learn if the candidate can be succinct while meeting a lesson goal.

Pre-observation Conference

After allowing adequate time for planning, invite the candidate for a ten- to fifteen-minute pre-observation conference. Similar to any clinical observation process, you use the pre-conference to:

- Clarify the lesson goal(s);
- Understand the context of the lesson;
- Discuss selected instructional methodology; and
- Determine how the prospective teacher will assess the success of the lesson.

The most important aspect of the pre-observation conference is that it provides a glimpse of the teacher's planning skills. During the conference, you can also determine how knowledgeable the person is about the latest best practices in instructional planning including the Common Core Standards.

Observation

The classroom observation should be conducted as soon as possible after the pre-observation conference. This tight timeframe is recommended to facilitate an efficient process. An effective strategy is to introduce the candidate to students as a visiting instructor. This will minimize student uncertainty and set the stage for the lesson.

Unlike a traditional observation with one of your regular faculty members, data collection and documentation are less formal. You and any other administrators conducting the observation should use the observation to form general impressions about the teacher's potential effectiveness. You might prepare a lesson rubric, which includes the key items such as:

- Ability to build rapport;
- Communication skills;
- Lesson goal attainment;
- Content area knowledge;
- Teaching style;
- Pacing;
- Student management; and
- Closure.

Rubric items should be specific to the position and grade level.

Through the demonstration lesson, you will quickly discover if the candidate can relate naturally with students. You will also develop a better understanding of the person's teaching style. This will help you make a much more informed hiring decision.

Post-Observation Conference

Closely following the observation, it is important to meet with the prospective teacher to process the experience. Similar to other steps in the process, a brief fifteen-minute post-observation conference is recommended.

Unlike a traditional post-observation conference, which is a collaborative, reflective conversation, these are more candidate-focused. Instead of giving feedback, you use the time to elicit as much as you can about the candidate's perspectives on teaching and learning. You want to understand the candidate's thinking as well as assess the person's self-reflection skills.

Here are sample questions you can use to focus the post-observation conference.

- How would you assess the success of your lesson?
- Why did you choose the teaching approach you did?
- Did you observe any students who appeared to need support?
- Did anything occur that surprised you?
- What was it that you did that was most effective?
- Given what occurred during the lesson, what would you do tomorrow?
- If you taught the lesson again, would you do anything differently?

As part of the discussion, you should probe candidate responses. If at all possible, be objective rather than judgmental.

As you facilitate the demonstration lesson, remember that this experience is stressful for any candidate. Common courtesy is to compliment at least two highlights of the teacher's performance and offer thanks for participating. Also, at the end of the post-conference, you should indicate when the final decision will be made. You should also let candidates know when they will be notified.

After the candidate leaves, you should immediately take time to discuss the teacher's performance with others who participated. Their assessments will help you clarify your thinking on the candidate. They may also identify points that you may not have otherwise considered.

Making the Final Decision

Hiring is not an exact science. Even if you plan and implement a comprehensive process, you may still hire a below average performer. However, by rigorously adhering to the process discussed, remaining as objective as possible, and weighing all the information gathered, you can significantly improve your hiring success. Just as important, you can take comfort in knowing that you have left no stone unturned.

Communication Tracking

A challenge all administrators experience is communicating with all applicants who are not selected for a position. Today, with the availability of online application software, this can be managed more efficiently than ever. You generally are able to create templates that can be automatically personalized for any position. Also, by using the software fully, you will be able to maintain electronic records, which may become important if any hiring issues are raised in the future. If you do not have access to an online application system, you can use Google Docs to track and schedule candidates.

POINTS TO REMEMBER

One of the most critical responsibilities administrators have is selecting outstanding teachers. As the school's leader, though, you will face numerous roadblocks which can interfere with the teacher selection. However, by implementing a comprehensive teacher selection process, you can overcome these challenges and increase the number of outstanding teachers you hire.

As you design your process, it is important to ensure that you identify a broad applicant pool including minority candidates. You must also build in multiple levels of interviews, each of which are structured for a specific purpose in the process. Prior to the final interview, conduct both informal and formal reference checking to help ensure your due diligence. Once a final candidate or two is identified, a demonstration teaching step will help you hone in on your preferred selection. By placing a top priority on teacher hiring, you will significantly increase your chances for hiring the most outstanding teachers available.

THREE

Fostering Novice Teacher Success

Each fall, a crop of newly hired teachers begins their new careers. Fresh-faced and eager, they arrive excited to have landed their first teaching job. They are motivated to make a difference. However, the initial euphoria can quickly disappear as day-to-day job pressures settle in.

Similar to the excitement that new teachers experience, administrators, too, are hopeful that these new hires will make a difference in their schools. Administrators know that an infusion of new teachers can have a positive and lasting effect on the school culture.

At the same time, beginning teacher success is often more a function of chance than planning. Unlike other careers that offer lengthy internships and direct supervision from veteran colleagues, most teachers find themselves alone in their classrooms. Traditionally, they are assigned the same job responsibilities and performance expectations on their first day of work as their most experienced colleagues. Unfortunately, typically they often do not receive the level of support and guidance needed to succeed.

Is it any wonder that many of these teachers struggle initially and some ultimately decide to leave the profession? Although teaching can be a very lonely and isolating career, the most successful principals understand this reality. As such, they build in school support systems designed to increase the success rate of first-year teachers. They never leave teacher development to chance.

These administrators recognize that the type and level of support new hires receive directly impacts their success and leads to higher student academic performance (Fullan, 2008). Highly effective administrators know how essential it is to help these novices bridge the gap between the knowledge and skills learned in teacher preparation programs and the realities of actual classroom instruction. They also recognize that failing to do so contributes to job dissatisfaction and faculty turnover.

As your school's leader, you will have invested substantial time, energy, and resources into the hiring process. It is in your best interest to do everything possible to ensure that your new teachers succeed. Otherwise, you will find yourself with a revolving door of new hires. The best way to avoid this cycle is to develop effective support systems. These will help increase the success rate of your new teachers especially during their all important first year.

Before developing effective support systems, it is important first to understand the developmental stages through which almost all new faculty members pass. This information will assist you as you design support systems that make a real difference in first-year teacher success and ultimately their retention.

STAGES OF NEW TEACHER DEVELOPMENT

A teacher's first year can feel like an emotional roller-coaster ride. Many "feel alone, bewildered, inadequate, resentful, oscillating between self blame, castigating the system, and blaming the irrelevance of much that they had experienced and been told in their preparatory programs" (Sarason, 1993, p. 57). In fact, the first year of teaching produces more highs and lows than any other year. One reason is that new teachers do not have the advantage of prior experience. They cannot put things into perspective as well as veterans.

The New Teacher Center (Santa Cruz, California) has been researching and supporting new teachers for over twenty years. In the early 1990s, Ellen Moir, director of the New Teacher Center, identified the phases of first-year teacher development as part of her work with the California Department of Education. According to Moir (2011), new teachers move through five stages.

Phase 1: Anticipation

While not every new teacher experiences the first year in the same way, most begin the school year full of excitement and anticipation. At the same time, they tend to glamorize their new position by focusing primarily on the perceived positives. Seldom do they initially consider all the challenges they will likely face.

Phase 2: Survival

Within a few weeks, the initial excitement is often tempered by reality. They may become overwhelmed with day-to-day demands. They also discover the mundane routines, which are ever present. These include a never-ending stream of papers to grade, lessons to plan, and parent phone calls to return. It is during this phase that their initial excitement is soon replaced with a desire for survival.

Phase 3: Disillusionment

As they move through the survival phase, they tend to experience a drop in energy and enthusiasm. Before long, they begin to question their personal efficacy. Some even wonder if they have what it takes to be a great teacher. Survival becomes the all-consuming focus. By November, it is common for feelings of disillusionment to creep in. For many, the end of the school year seems very far away.

Phase 4: Rejuvenation

For many of these beginning professionals, winter vacation cannot come too soon. The break from the day-to-day teaching responsibilities and the chance to relax can restore energy. The time away from teaching also adds perspective. For some, this marks the beginning of the rejuvenation phase. For others, though, it may still be a month or two away. In any event, it is during this phase that many experience a renewed sense of commitment. They also begin to develop coping strategies that help them gather much-needed perspective.

Phase 5: Reflection

The final phase is reflection, which typically emerges by early spring. At this point, many new teachers find themselves better equipped to reflect more honestly upon their year. It is during this phase that they reach a point where they can put teaching realities into perspective. Once they do so, they are ready to develop personal coping skills to temper the daily peaks and valleys so inherent in teaching. It is also the time when they know they have finally transitioned from college student to teaching professional.

Not all teachers, however, transition through all of these stages. Those who do not ultimately either leave the profession, are released from employment, or never progress to the level of reflective practitioner.

As principal, it is critical for you to recognize these phases of beginning teacher development, especially as you design new teacher support systems. If you do not, you will miss an opportunity to help develop a highly effective teaching staff. You will also increase your chances of experiencing a revolving door of teacher hires.

ORIENTATION AND INDUCTION

Preparing beginning teachers for the realities of their position is not simple. It involves more than handing them the keys to their classrooms and a lesson on how the copier works. As the school leader, you need to design a professional development plan to get them off to a smooth start. You should include two essential components in your plan: orientation and induction.

Orientation

Orientation is the process through which you ensure that new teachers are familiar with the school-community culture as well as district norms and expectations. Without a solid foundation, most beginners will spend weeks trying to self-discover information, which could have been provided upfront.

To begin your orientation planning, remember that it is essential to allow adequate time for what you want to accomplish. Too often principals and other central office administrators clog orientation activities with district-focused priorities or too much routine paperwork. While these are important, they should be managed in as efficient a way as possible to target what new teachers need most for a successful start.

One of the most important decisions you will make is what you choose to include in your new teacher orientation activities. Another is when and how you deliver these. Here are several strategies you should consider.

Strategy 1: Maximize use of the time between hiring and their first day on the job.   With proper planning, you can accomplish a great deal before new teachers assume their positions. New teachers are eager to absorb information about the school and district. Here are several suggestions to maximize available time.

- Provide teachers with a set of professional books to read over the summer. Select those that support key school or district philosophies or initiatives. Some districts even provide guiding questions to help focus new teachers' learning.
- Have co-workers reach out to beginning teachers. Encourage veteran teachers to invite them for coffee or lunch.
- Invite new teachers to participate in appropriate summer professional development activities that are scheduled for staff. These include training and curriculum writing projects. Not only will they learn important information, they will start to feel a part of the faculty.
- Invite them to specific summer training designed for them. Too often administrators wait until the school year starts to begin orien-

tation activities. Beginning teachers will benefit far more from orientation when they do not feel the pressures of the first day of school.

- Offer training through online or podcast formats. These allow new hires to learn important information at their own pace during the summer. This is an efficient way to inform them, especially about policies, procedures, and organizational tasks. This will help maximize the limited time you have available once the school year officially begins. Such an approach will allow you to focus on more complex activities during district-required orientation time.

Strategy 2: Develop written materials that provide essential information. Put documents and other important information such as the faculty handbook or curriculum guides online. These should be stored in the "staff only" section of your school or district website. You might personalize some to be grade level or department specific. Other items you might include are:

- A "welcome" from the principal or department chair;
- School schedules;
- Calendar with dates and deadlines;
- School-specific discipline policies and procedures;
- Grading procedures; and
- A "who's who" picture directory of building staff.

Strategy 3: Design group activities that build relationships. Often overlooked during orientation is the opportunity for the new teachers to get to know each other and the broader community. Here are several suggested activities you can use to allow teachers to get to know each other and the community while building faculty relationships.

- Conduct a "treasure hunt." New teachers work in pairs or teams to gather facts about the community, district, and school. As they complete this task, meet with them to discuss what they learned. Through this simple activity, they will develop a better understanding of the community while getting to know each other. The "treasure list" could include: types of businesses, public services, transportation, socioeconomic makeup of the community, youth organizations, and historical facts.
- Schedule a meeting with new faculty members at your school prior to any scheduled district orientation activities. This will add a personal touch to orientation. It will also allow you to make them feel welcomed in your school immediately. This subtle but effective approach communicates the importance you place on relationships.
- Assign new teachers to cohort groups based on similar job assignments. Prior to doing so, work with your veteran faculty members to identify ways they can help new colleagues assimilate into core

school groups. Such an approach sets high school-wide expectations for collaboration.

Strategy 4: Use Quick Start Guides (QSGs) to increase orientation efficiency.   Items that traditionally take up orientation time but are not immediate needs can be managed more efficiently through technology. QSGs allow both beginning and current faculty members easy access to important information anywhere at any time. QSGs usually contain screen shots or other visuals with step-by-step directions, which reside on the district intranet. By providing simplified step-by-step directions for routine duties, you can save valuable orientation time by using QSGs. Sample topics to address include:

- Accessing your online paycheck;
- Securing a substitute teacher;
- Setting up your email account;
- Setting up your voice mailbox; and
- Taking student attendance.

To further increase efficiency, you might suggest that new teachers bookmark the documents they will use regularly. In this way, they will know where to look quickly when they need information.

Strategy 5: Vary orientation activity formats to improve the quality of meeting time.   Consider "flipping" the orientation format by asking the new teachers to read materials or view a podcast prior to your first meeting with them. For example, if you want to ensure that they understand Common Core Standards, provide then with a web-based video beforehand so they arrive better prepared for orientation discussions. By reversing the traditional format of presenting information first then asking them to study it later, you can make better use of limited available time. You also make orientation conversation more meaningful while enhancing their learning.

As you design your orientation activities, keep in mind that beginning teachers crave information about their new school. They want to know the schedule, rituals, and traditions. They also want to know how student behavior is managed and what supports are in place to assist them. They need to understand the communication structures and where to go for information. By carefully designing your new teacher orientation program, your beginning faculty members will feel more fully informed. You will also help them begin to connect with members of the faculty.

Induction

One mistake administrators make is thinking that induction and orientation are synonymous. As a result, they build orientation activities into induction programs rather than separating them. Induction is best described as providing new teachers with the "nuts and bolts" of their professional responsibilities. Induction addresses such questions as:

- How do I use the copier?
- How do I take attendance?
- What do I do during a fire or emergency drill?
- What is the format for parent-teacher conferences?
- How do I submit my report card grades?

In some schools where such topics are not discussed during orientation. Learning this information is often left to chance. Beginning teachers must seek out routine information themselves. This can be time consuming and very inefficient.

To increase induction efficiency, you must prepare an induction plan. Ideally, it should be formalized and structured. Think of induction more as a year-long process rather than a meeting or two at the beginning of the year. The most effective principals schedule induction sessions throughout the year. They think through what faculty members need to do on a quarterly or even more regular basis. Some even link their plans to key events such as the opening of school, open house night, parent curriculum evening, parent conferencing, school budgeting, or similar items.

To design a comprehensive new teacher induction program, consider the following strategies.

Strategy 1: Do your homework. A good way to identify the most relevant induction topics is to survey second-, third-, and fourth-year teachers. Simply ask them to identify topics that would have helped them during their initial year of employment. Also, probe them for their suggestions on presentation timing. Typical initial year induction topics include:

- School keys and security;
- Open house or curriculum nights formats and expectations;
- Homework policies;
- Parent-teacher conference structure and expectations;
- Report cards and grading expectations;
- Standardized testing schedules and requirements;
- All-school or grade level events as well as field trip and assembly procedures;
- Classroom parties and event procedures;
- Specialized student services (for example, special education, English Language Learners or "ELL," gifted);
- Classroom organization for school breaks and summer; and
- Supply requisition procedures for the next school year.

Strategy 2: Set a schedule of meetings. Establishing an effective induction program does not have to be complicated. It can be as simple as creating a schedule of new teacher meetings throughout the year. These meetings could be planned before or after school, or even over lunch. In setting the schedule, you should attempt to time the meetings and topics addressed to coincide with specific school deadlines and events. Make sure you keep in mind the stages of first-year teacher development.

Strategy 3: Select master teachers to assist with induction activities.   Induction activities are a great way to engage veteran teachers in supporting their newest colleagues. Once you have developed a meeting schedule with selected topics, feel free to invite other teachers to participate especially as panel members. By carefully selecting veteran teachers to serve as experts during these sessions, you can be sure that beginning teachers receive accurate information. You will also establish important connections between new staff members and well-respected veterans.

Strategy 4: Use discussion with veteran teachers and role-playing to better prepare beginning teachers for situations they will face during their initial year.   New teachers may not even know what they do not know. Universities and teacher preparation programs prepare them well for instruction and lesson design, but usually not as thoroughly for many other teacher job responsibilities. One way to bridge the gap from teacher preparation and on-the-job performance is to build in opportunities for them to learn from their experienced colleagues.

To do this, invite veteran faculty members to not only identify their most important responsibilities but also to provide advice on how best to handle each. To further support new staff, build in activities that lend themselves to role-playing.

Listed below are sample role-play topics you might consider.

- Conducting parent-teacher conferences.
- Managing various administrative tasks.
- Completing report cards.
- Establishing homework expectations.
- Dealing with a difficult parent or student.

Strategy 5: Lead all aspects of the induction program yourself if at all possible.   One mistake building-level administrators make is turning over induction to either central office personnel or teachers. New faculty will associate you more directly as their school leader if you are an active participant in all induction activities. Your involvement will also provide "quality control." What you say and do strongly influences new teacher thinking while setting high performance expectations. Ultimately, through induction, you can directly promote your school's overall culture and climate through your actions and words.

Your overall teacher induction goal is to help beginning teachers succeed. A highly structured and well-developed teacher induction program will provide them with the information and tools they need to get off to a positive start. It will also help your begin the process of acculturating new teachers to your school. Just as importantly, you will likely improve beginning teacher retention while making their first year a more satisfying one.

POINTS TO REMEMBER

Supporting new teachers in their first years is a key to successfully building a highly effective teaching staff. Understanding the developmental stages new teachers experience will provide you with information essential to developing an effective beginning teacher support system. Also, remember that comprehensive orientation and induction programs will increase your chances of ensuring that new hires will have a successful and satisfying first teaching year.

FOUR

Building a Comprehensive Mentoring Program

Even with the best orientation and induction plan, new teachers will benefit further from participation in a well-planned mentoring program. Through mentoring, novice teachers receive the support they need to develop as professional educators. Mentoring programs bridge the gap between preservice learning and the requirements of the job itself. They assist beginning teachers in developing the knowledge, skills, and confidence they need to build a long, successful career.

Mentoring, though, is not exclusively for new teachers. Experienced faculty members who have changed districts or schools or teach at a different grade level often require some support. Quality mentoring programs can address the needs of both inexperienced and experienced teachers by differentiating the level of support provided to match their individual needs. Mentoring further provides administrators with the opportunity to help teachers understand cultural norms, which are influenced by school, district, and administrative expectations.

When mentor programs were originally initiated years ago, they typically focused on partnering new teachers with veteran "buddies." The role of the mentor was to provide cookies and Kleenex tissues and lend a shoulder for inexperienced teachers to lean on when the job became tough. Mentors also often brightened a new teacher's day with a gift. This was a nice gesture, but did little to improve a new teacher's effectiveness. These are still responsibilities of mentors and should be encouraged. However, they are only a very small part of a mentor's role.

Today, mentor programs focus less on feel-good "fluff" and more on instructional coaching. Teacher candidates no longer ask, "Do you have a mentoring program?" Instead, they ask administrators to describe their mentoring programs. Beginning teachers expect to be partnered with instructional mentors who will support them toward becoming successful teachers.

High-performing principals understand that mentoring is much more than simply pairing up buddies. Principals work to match new teachers with trained, respected veterans. They view these professional relationships as more than cursory. These principals leverage the resources available to them to develop programs that include very well-articulated components. In larger districts, mentoring may be part of a district program, which is supported through district resources.

Regardless of whether programs are solely school-based or part of a broader district effort, quality mentoring programs include components such as self-assessment of teaching, shared reflection, data conversations, observation, and feedback, all focused on student learning. These programs are typically built on a clear purpose, comprehensive mentor training, and ongoing formative assessment.

Failing to provide a comprehensive new teacher mentoring program can come with a cost. New teachers who do not receive early support are more likely to experience job dissatisfaction and leave their positions for a more supportive environment or even another profession. They also are less effective in the classrooms than they could be.

PHASES OF MENTORING RELATIONSHIPS

Before discussing how to design an effective mentoring program, it is important to consider the phases of the mentoring relationship. A successful mentoring relationship evolves in a predictable manner. It begins with the establishment of the relationship between the mentor and the mentee. As the relationship develops, the mentor's role changes, which allows greater mentee independence through a gradual release of support. Finally, in a successful relationship the mentor becomes a critical partner in joint professional inquiry. It is at this point that the new teacher reaches a level of independence and is firmly established as a reflective practitioner.

Kram (1983) categorizes these four phases of mentoring.

- Initiation: the period of becoming acquainted with each other. During this stage, mentors and new teachers get to know each other. Trust is built during this phase of the relationship. New teachers begin to view mentors as helpful supporters while mentors assess new teachers' needs.
- Cultivation: developing the relationship to focus on promoting and enhancing teaching and learning. As the relationship develops, trust is firmly established. Beginning teachers become comfortable sharing the ups and downs of teaching with their mentors who help focus conversations on instruction.

- Separation: the intentional diminishing of mentor support and increasing of independence for the mentee. At some point in the relationship, mentors begin to scale back their directive role. This is an important step in helping new teachers achieve independence. During the initiation and cultivation stages, new teachers develop a dependence on their mentors. During the separation phase, mentors focus on monitoring their relationships with mentees and intentionally diminish overt support. This allows mentees to begin to establish their personal teaching identities. Just as important, mentors must recognize that they are not creating clones of themselves.
- Redefinition: the evolution of the relationship to peer coaching or critical friend. At this point, new teachers begin to establish a level of independence. They are able to identify more meaningful professional and instructional goals. Mentors no longer solely guide their joint conversations. Instead, new teachers turn to the mentors for assistance in professional inquiry.

Although these phases can span more than the first year, effective mentors understand that their goal is to work themselves out of a job. Ultimately, they need to help beginning teachers become effective, confident professionals who no longer require direct mentorship but rather more informal assistance from a peer coach or critical friend.

DESIGNING AND IMPLEMENTING YOUR MENTORING PROGRAM

An effective mentoring program is purposeful and intentional, which means that it requires extensive planning. As such, it is important for you to begin the planning process by identifying key questions that you will need to consider as you develop your mentoring program framework. The New Teacher Center (Goldrick et al., 2012), which has conducted an extensive review of state mentoring programs, suggests that you should consider the following questions.

- Will your program be designed to address just those in their first two years in the profession or also experienced teachers new to your district?
- What will be your program goals?
- What resources are available to support the program?
- How will the program be structured on a day-to-day basis?
- What will be your mentor program coordinator's responsibilities?
- How will you recruit your mentor program coordinator?
- What will be the primary job responsibilities of your mentors?
- How will you select your mentors?
- How will you train your mentors?
- What will be your expectations for program participants?

- What types of common experiences (observations, coaching, feedback) will you build into your program?
- What will be your ongoing system of program review?

Will your program be designed to address just those in their first two years in the profession or also experienced teachers new to your district? Not every teacher you hire is a new college graduate. Some of your new hires arrive with prior teaching experience. Others may be changing schools or grade levels, and still some may bring life experiences from prior careers. As you design your program, you need to keep in mind the teachers' backgrounds. A flexible versus rigid program will allow you to tailor each mentee's experience to their specific needs.

New college graduates require different levels of support. In addition to learning how to be successful faculty members, they also must transition into the work world. Tax forms, insurance choices, licensure, and retirement are foreign to recent graduates. They may also need guidance in creating a separation between their personal and professional lives.

New teachers who are not recent college graduates, typically mid-career changers, require less support to understand the world of work or to find a balance between their personal and professional life. However, they may still need assistance in understanding such areas as licensure or pension systems that are unique to education.

Teachers who bring prior teaching experience to their new positions often require support to understand and fit into their new district and school cultures. They need less emphasis on developing their teaching identity and understanding the work world. Instead they require more emphasis on school and district policies and procedures. They also must learn how to apply what they already know to their new setting.

Often forgotten during mentoring are district teachers who are changing buildings, grade levels, departments, or assignments. These teachers need support specific to their new roles. This may include training in specific instructional materials, reporting student progress, or applying specific school-wide programs. They also may require assistance learning the culture of their team, department, or building.

It is useful to analyze your hiring pattern by looking back at the teachers you have hired during the past five years. Review their education level, prior teaching experience, and other nonteaching experience. Look for patterns to help guide you in developing a program that will meet the needs of your typical hires. As you build that program, maintain flexibility to address future needs.

What will be your program goals? In addition to addressing the varying needs of teachers new to your building, one of the most important factors in any successful mentoring program is clearly defining program goals. To begin the goal setting process, research the latest best practices in the field. Just as most curricular areas have standards, so do mentoring programs. Most states have their own set of mentoring standards. A simple search on the Internet will lead you to the various states' standards. If your state does not have standards, you should seek out those from other states. This is a good place to start your research. It is also useful to reach out to other school districts that have successful mentoring programs and ask them for information.

Interviewing your newer teachers, those in their first three to five years in your district, is another strategy to help you understand beginning teachers' needs. This information will assist you in guiding your program development. Ask them to think back to when they started in the district and identify what they wish they had known. Also ask them what they found most helpful during their first year. These insights will prove valuable in defining your program goals.

After completing your initial research phase, ask yourself three questions, which will assist you in finalizing program goals.

- Who is the mentoring program designed to serve?
- What are the main objectives of the mentoring program?
- How will we use your mentor program to encourage new teachers to become reflective practitioners?

What resources are available to support the program? Once you have established your program goals, your next step is to identify adequate resources to achieve them. Begin by exploring resources (time and money) available in your school district. Your central office administrators can assist. Many times, local educational foundations as well as parent organizations value contributing to teacher development programs that may benefit their children. You may also discover that your school board will support your request through additional funding. Before pursuing these options, it is wise to consult with your district superintendent for advice and support.

When resources are tight or you work in a small school district with minimal support personnel, you may need to become especially creative. This may mean scheduling mentoring sessions and planning meetings over lunch or before school rather than as paid activities. Sometimes principals or nonteaching staff (for example, librarian, psychologist) will volunteer to substitute for classes to facilitate meetings or activities such as peer classroom observations. At other times, you may need to employ creative substitute teacher scheduling to provide time for program participants to meet program goals. These are just some of the creative ways administrators find resources to make mentoring a reality.

How will the program be structured on a day-to-day basis? Once you have identified whom you will serve, your program goals, and the resources available to you, you are ready to define your day-to-day program. Often districts establish an expected number of annual hours that mentors and mentees will meet. They may even identify the frequency (for example, at least once every other week). These should be defined at the start of the program so that everyone knows what is expected. A typical program includes approximately fifteen hours of meetings throughout the year. Participants are expected to commit to either a one-year or two-year program upfront. Remember that mentors and their new teachers may require your guidance to find designated time to meet throughout the year.

You will want to establish forms for meeting notes and logs to document meetings. Procedures should also be developed and may be included in your mentoring handbook or other guide. These forms and procedures will help to organize the mentor to ensure program consistency.

Mentoring is a challenging assignment, and your mentors need support, too. Opportunities for mentors to meet with other mentors to compare strategies, review protocols, and share ideas should also be a program expectation. Time should be allotted for mentors to meet together to discuss common concerns and challenges. Such meetings help ensure program accountability.

You will also want to outline specific topics to be discussed. An effective approach is to establish an annual calendar listing each. While informal discussions and spontaneous interactions are invaluable, certain activities between mentors and new teachers must be intentional and planned. This calendar can guide the mentor while ensuring that key topics such as open house, parent conferences, report cards, and budgeting are addressed.

In addition to personalized mentoring, some districts offer topic-specific in-house courses. These high-quality courses are taught by mentors, other teachers, or even members of the administrative staff. The range of topics is almost endless but can be tied to district and building priorities. Some may be targeted to beginners and others to those with some experience. Through participation in courses, new teachers build collegiality with colleagues while creating a learning community. Consider building in "essential" classes that teach about the specific district culture, community, and philosophy. Also, you might offer "elective" classes tied to curricular initiatives or district/building goals that may be of interest to veteran teachers as well.

What will be your mentor program coordinator's responsibilities?
For your mentor program to succeed, you must assign one person who is responsible for the overall program. This is usually a mentor program coordinator. With clear leadership, you will increase the likelihood that your program will become institutionalized. However, to do this, you must clearly delineate the coordinator's responsibilities. These will vary from school to school. Here are several that are common to most mentoring programs.

- Encouraging and inviting new teachers to seek a mentor, if the program is optional. In some states and districts, participation in mentoring is required and the coordinator simply provides program information to new teachers.
- Gathering information about new teachers in order to carefully match each to an available mentor.
- Collecting forms from participants to verify that the program is being implemented consistently.
- Training new mentors using the district and/or state mentoring curriculum.
- Planning and conducting support meetings with mentees.
- Troubleshooting mentors' or mentees' concerns.
- Planning and conducting meetings for active mentors.
- Designing annual training for mentors and mentees.
- Overseeing program from beginning to completion.

How will you recruit your mentor program coordinator? Once you have defined the program coordinator responsibilities, you are ready for the next crucial decision, selection of your coordinator. Hopefully, you will have at least one staff member with the skills, initiative, and personal qualities necessary.

To begin the selection process, solicit interest from those who you believe would be most effective. It is insufficient to merely post the position and hope a good candidate applies. If you do, you may not identify your best leader. Teachers are often reluctant to put themselves in a position of leadership with other faculty members. However, if recruited and encouraged, they may decide to do so. Before starting the recruitment process, make sure that you discuss your plan as well as potential candidates with your superintendent and/or central office administrators. They can advise you on roadblocks you may face or teacher contract issues. They also may have strong opinions about those you are considering.

Begin by meeting with those you are recruiting as well as anyone else who expresses interest. Those considering applying need to understand the position requirements and your expectations. This meeting will provide you with a vehicle to "sell" the role to the right person.

When recruiting candidates, consider those who you believe have the ability to clearly articulate the program goals and who have already demonstrated school or district leadership. These individuals should be positive supporters of school and district initiatives. In addition, look for individuals who are organized, comfortable with problem solving, and confident. They also must possess strong interpersonal skills as well as an understanding of how to foster a vision for the future of the program. Finally, the coordinator should be someone who works well with others.

As part of the recruitment process, it is important to emphasize the need for the coordinator to possess a keen understanding of the balance between confidentiality and an obligation to share information with the administration. Coordinators are similar to social workers who build a trusting confidential relationship with others while recognizing when something needs to be shared with administrators.

What will be the primary job responsibilities of your mentors? As was true with the program coordinator, defining the specific job responsibilities of your mentors is very important. For a mentor/mentee relationship to flourish, both must be on the same page. If not, your program will become more perfunctory than dynamic. Below are several primary mentor responsibilities that are common to well-functioning programs.

- Assisting teachers in refining their instructional skills.
- Using questioning to guide new teachers to reflect on performance.
- Describing the "thinking of teaching" to assist new faculty members in understanding the decision-making and planning that goes into teaching.
- Serving as a critical observer, supporter, and encourager.
- Providing direct performance feedback in an encouraging and supportive manner.
- Encouraging new colleagues to take appropriate instructional risks.
- Providing advice regarding professional conduct and school cultural norms.

How will you select your mentors? Before beginning your selection process, remember that your best teachers may not always be your most effective mentors. Teachers who are highly effective in the classroom may not be equally skilled working with adult colleagues. As a result, mentor selection means much more than picking popular, hardworking, supportive teachers. There is no question that effective mentors must be excellent teachers. However, they must be equally effective when working with adults. They must also possess the skills, knowledge, and talents to lead adults while being viewed as positive influences in the district. They need to be supporters of school and district goals and initiatives and should be excited about the direction the district and school are heading.

Successful mentors also have a good grasp of adult learning theory, patience, and strong communication and observation skills. They remember what it was like to be a new teacher and display a sense of empathy. They recognize the importance of effective modeling while facilitating discussion rather than providing all the "answers." They see coaching and personal support as professional development tools.

To select your mentors, create an application process that will require candidates to show their interest while providing information useful for selection. Minimally, applicants should be asked to provide a resume of relevant professional activities that demonstrate leadership, participation in training, and commitment to the school and district. They should provide references who can speak to their qualifications for the position.

As the building administrator, you should lead the mentor selection process. At the least, you should include your mentor program coordinator but may also choose to involve key building teachers or other district administrators. Before selecting interview team members, though, make sure that you have considered your school's cultural norms. For example, if teachers are accustomed to being included, make sure that you honor this expectation.

In addition, it is important to maintain final authority for the selection, which means clarifying that you will make the final hiring decision. This will help facilitate more collaboration between your coordinator and the mentors. At the same time, you will be better positioned to ensure that the program remains true to its goals. Also, clearly define committee member roles so they know what is expected of them.

Once you have identified your interview team and mentor applicant pool, you are almost ready to interview candidates. However, before you do, you must to train your committee members on the selection process. One mistake you can make is simply assembling a group of interviewers and beginning the interview process with no preparation. To make sound selections, you must treat the mentor selection process much as you would a teacher hiring process. A poor selection now will doom the success of your program.

After developing the criteria for an ideal candidate, design a rubric for committee members to complete during the interviews. Rubrics are especially useful for focusing interviews and targeting key selection criteria. Such a process will increase the efficiency of the process and lead to better mentor choices.

How will you train your mentors?   A crucial element of any comprehensive mentoring program is mentor training. You must decide how best to provide them within the limitation of the size of your school and available resources. One approach to consider is contracting with an outside consultant who has the knowledge and skills to provide thorough in-house training. Some regional offices of education or states offer such programs. Another approach is to ask administrators from districts with successful programs how they prepared their mentors. Finally, if you do not have the resources to contract for consulting, training could be folded into the responsibilities of the mentor program coordinator.

No matter what approach you ultimately choose, you should consider including the following elements into your training curriculum.

- Understanding and applying the principles of adult learning.
- Understanding the stages of new teacher development.
- Building trust and confidence.

- Demonstrating active listening skills.
- Understanding best practices in mentoring.
- Developing coaching skills.
- Developing a foundational knowledge of research and best practices in increasing student achievement.
- Understanding and implementing the reflective clinical observation process.
- Recognizing effective instructional practices.
- Understanding and applying reflective questioning techniques.
- Addressing logistical concerns such as scheduling meetings, completing required forms, and developing a calendar of key topics to address.
- Role-playing conversations with a mentee.
- Practicing classroom observation.

As part of the development of your mentor training, you must determine the delivery format. Often, mentor training programs span at least two to three full days or four to five half days. At times, training is scheduled in the summer or as a series of after-school sessions. Other times, mentors are freed from teaching during the training period. Remember that no one approach fits all situations. However, you must establish a regular training schedule for thoroughness and continuity.

What will be your expectations for program participants? Program participants should clearly understand your expectations for their participation. Mentees need to be provided with information about the time commitment and any upcoming dates for group meetings. They need to be given information on expectations for scheduling meeting times with their mentors as well as completing any mandated forms. Most programs expect participants to log their hours. Others require mentees to develop personal professional development goals and/or maintain reflective journals. As you define your program, do not forget to clearly delineate your expectations for the participants.

What types of common experiences will you build into your program? It is important to build common experiences into your mentoring program. Without these, your program will lack continuity and increase the likelihood of it becoming fragmented. Although what you choose to include and how you plan to implement it vary from district to district, mentoring programs usually incorporate the following experiences.

- Extensive professional development linked to research-based teaching practices and data analysis.
- Direct classroom observations with feedback by the mentor.
- Reflective journaling.
- Opportunities for participants to observe each other as well as their mentors.

- Multiple opportunities for mentors and mentees to interact.

What will be your ongoing system of program review? For your mentor programming to remain viable and vibrant, you must build in systematic program review. Too often, administrators forget the importance of regular review. Instead, they see the program operating well and assume it will continue to do so.

Without constant oversight, your program can lose its initial momentum. Remember that administrators must assume responsibility for leading program review. If you do, you will better understand the needs of your participants and be well positioned to lead any needed program changes.

Feedback can be gathered in multiple ways. Listed below are several to consider.

- Devote some time at all meetings to solicit program participant feedback. Even just asking for others' opinions and suggestions will have a positive impact on program vitality.
- Survey current program participants and mentors individually. They may have ideas to share that they are uncomfortable discussing in the group setting.
- Survey or interview other district and building administrators, including your superintendent, for their perspectives.
- Review retention and turnover data following the first year of the program and follow up as warranted with participants.
- Meet at least annually with your program coordinator and mentors to review the program calendar, common elements, and professional development topics.
- Meet with your program coordinator to review the program structure and related documents and activities, especially in light of program assessment data you gathered.

This review process is extensive and can be time consuming. However, by committing to such a thorough review, you will have sound information upon which to make informal program adjustments. You will also subtly send the message to everyone in your school and district that you value teacher development.

POINTS TO REMEMBER

Each mentoring program is unique. While there are elements common to effective programs, there is no specific formula for success. It is important to tailor your program to meet your individual school and district needs. Remember, too, that supporting your new teachers cannot be left to chance. Simply matching a veteran teacher with the new teacher and hoping for the best is often no better than not having a program at all.

Effective mentoring programs must be intentional and well planned. There must have specific goals and protocols. Finally, the goal of every mentoring program is to make sure our new teachers are provided the best training and experiences possible to help them to develop into master teachers.

FIVE

Raising the Supervision Bar

Evidence supporting the importance of principal leadership in improving schools and increasing student learning is clear (Marzano, Waters, and McNulty, 2005). Effective principals make a difference. What they say and do has a significant impact on the school's culture as well as how teachers and staff perform. In fact, how well they supervise others is a critical factor in their leadership success.

To appreciate this point, consider these questions. Have you ever visited a school and, within a few minutes, developed a good sense of the school atmosphere? After meeting the principal, did the school's culture tend to reflect the personality and priorities of the principal? If so, your experience is not unusual.

Because principals have such an impact on their schools, how well they perform their supervision responsibilities is critical to school success and ultimately student learning. How they choose to spend their time and how much they focus on effective supervision often defines the school's culture. More importantly, their supervisory leadership directly impacts the school's overall effectiveness.

Unfortunately, some school principals are ineffective supervisors. They either fail to be proactive leaders or act in ways that are detrimental to school improvement. Through their actions and/or inactions, they fail to raise the supervision bar. On the other hand, the most effective supervisors understand how to be strong leaders. Through their daily supervision, they are difference makers. Discussed below are four strategies, which you may want to consider to ramp up your supervisory effectiveness.

Strategy 1: Be decisive. Some principals are afraid to make unpopular decisions. What they fail to recognize is that the decisions by strong leaders are often questioned. Weak leaders worry more about how others will react rather than whether their decisions are correct. Remember, too, that even though some stakeholders may react negatively to certain decisions, they do not expect school leaders to make only popular decisions.

Because of fear, less effective principals actually make themselves irrelevant by avoiding difficult decision-making. Those who ignore problems rather than address them directly often lose the respect of others. More importantly, they only postpone issues, which will eventually surface. At the same time, their inaction communicates lower performance expectations for all staff.

Principals who are highly respected supervisors make decisions based on what is in the best interests of the students, school, and district. They understand the value of decisiveness. Rather than either ignoring problems or procrastinating, they are proactive decision-makers.

This does not mean that they are arbitrary, capricious, or thoughtless. Rather, they take time to weigh all factors without permitting personal considerations to overly influence their decisions. If this means rating an ineffective veteran teacher as "In Need of Improvement," even though the decision may be unpopular with staff and parents, they do so.

Strategy 2: Place relationship building at the top of your supervision priorities. Strong administrators recognize the power of relationships. They understand that they can accomplish much more if those they supervise respect them as individuals as well as administrators.

Some principals though undermine their own success by hiding behind formalities. Have you even worked with administrators who were so formal that they required others to address them as "Mr.," "Mrs.," "Ms.," or "Dr."? Such formality sets relationship barriers while discouraging collegiality.

Still others create barriers between themselves and staff members by limiting their access to them. For example, they require staff members to schedule appointments through office personnel just to meet with them. Such limits can quickly dampen any relationship.

Finally, a few administrators operate on the premise that if they are too open with subordinates, they cannot be effective supervisors. They worry that if they are too close with employees, their ability to discipline them will be compromised. As a consequence, they purposely establish superficial personal relationships. Unfortunately, others will recognize such artificiality quickly.

To build strong relationships with your staff, consider the following approaches.

- Maintain a true open-door policy. Some principals say that they have an open-door policy but do not demonstrate it. Just saying you do without doing it hurts rather than builds relationships. Symbolically, it is important to ensure that your door is literally open. This simple action says volumes about you. Avoid the temptation to close your office door even if you experience regular interruptions. The key is finding a balance that works for you. These drop-in moments for staff, parents, and even students are relationship builders.

- Make every effort to appear calm and relaxed even when you are not. Principals always feel rushed. They experience the pressure of immediate priorities as well as dilemmas that are not easily resolved. Even in the face of demands, if you are patient, others will feel more comfortable around you. You will also encourage rather than discourage others to seek you out.

- Avoid allowing others to distract you when you are having a conversation with someone, a common frustration of many. It is courteous to acknowledge their presence with a simple glance or hand gesture. However, avoid letting them interrupt the flow of the conversation until appropriate.

- Silence phones and ignore laptop communication when meeting with others. Responding to either will annoy others and hurt your relationships.

- Make sure that you honor your commitments to others. They will trust you more if you stay true to your word. Sometimes, though, circumstances may change. If so, make sure you explain what happened. They may not agree with you but will respect your honesty.

- Look for opportunities to interact informally with staff members. This may include stopping into classrooms or staff offices during noninstructional times. It might mean dropping into the staff lounge during typical break or lunch periods without any purpose other than conversation. Although this sounds simple, too often busy administrators focus exclusively on other responsibilities and forget the value of socializing. However, be cautious that you are not overly friendly or too social, which can have a detrimental effect on relationships.

- Avoid showing favoritism. You will always have certain teachers, support staff, students, or parents with whom you feel more connected. Unfortunately, a sure way to undermine your school relationships is to show any favoritism. Principals who present themselves as equalitarian are more trusted and respected. Once others perceive you as having favorites, their confidence in you will be diminished.

- Look for ways to praise staff in as nonpublic a manner as possible. A natural tendency of any administrator is to publicly recognize individuals for their contributions and successes. This, though, can create jealousies among others. A better approach is to recognize successes on a personal level through individual contact or written thank you notes. Another is to compliment their efforts to district administrators who at some point will probably mention to them that you said something positive about them.

Strategy 3: Be visible. Principals can easily become office-bound. If they are not careful, they will find themselves held captive by even those things that they can control. One is technology. As the role of technology in every facet of school life has grown, so too has the temptation to be glued to the computer, laptop, tablet, or smart phone. It is easy to continuously check email and text messages or to generate unnecessary written communication. These, of course, are important in moderation and can increase personal and organizational efficiency. However, equating time at your computer with productive work time can be a mistake. Those who do may be perceived as office-bound and out of touch.

To counter this, you should focus on personal visibility. You never want to be the principal who walks into a classroom and students ask who you are! Rather, you want others to see you as a fixture in the school community.

A simple but effective way to increase your day-to-day visibility is to commit regular time to stepping out of your office and leaving your electronic devices behind. Such an approach will make you informally accessible. Simply position yourself at key locations in the school during times when others are naturally transitioning between activities. This will allow students, staff, and even visitors to interact informally with you. These might include greeting students and parents during arrival and dismissal. You should also "stake out" various spots in the hallway during passing periods where others know where to find you. You will be amazed just how much business you can conduct during these times reaching out.

Another approach is to schedule meetings in teachers' rooms. Going to them rather than asking them to come to you increases your visibility with not only the teacher but others who see you.

Strategy 4: Increase your classroom presence. Teachers have long considered their classrooms their personal arenas. They believe that they should be able to walk into their classrooms, close their doors, and do what they want to do. Many consider supervisory comments from administrators as something to be tolerated rather than desired. This perception has grown out of decades of school leadership focused more on management efficiency than educational improvement.

Although this relationship between roles has begun to change in recent years, some teachers still view administrators more as managers than mentors. As a result, it is common for new administrators to find the instructional expertise for which they were admired when they taught suddenly ignored by teachers. Even those who were highly respected as teachers may find their teaching expertise minimized when they step into administration. What this means for you as a new administrator is that you must earn your instructional leadership credentials.

How do you establish your "street" credibility especially with teachers? One is to step up your supervision. One supervision activity you can use to earn respect as an instructional leader while enhancing your supervisory effectiveness is daily rounds.

Daily Rounds

A simple yet effective technique to increase your presence in classrooms is the daily rounds. Too often administrators forget to make classroom visitation a priority. Because they are stretched from all sides, it is easy for them to get caught up in the daily activity of the school.

Increasing your classroom "face time" begins by setting a visitation goal. For example, commit to dropping into three or four classrooms each day. You can decide how best to accomplish this in your personal situation. The key is making a specific commitment and sticking with it. Once you fall into this routine, it will become automatic.

What makes these visits doable is that they last for only a minute or two. However, before starting, ensure that your faculty members know that you will be regularly visiting their classrooms. Let them know that these visits help you stay in touch with daily instruction.

When conducting daily rounds, you are not normally expected to document visits or even informally meet with teachers. Make sure, though, that your district or state does not require it. Some states, such as Illinois, mandate documentation for any problems that are identified as part of the teacher evaluation process. Even if not mandatory, you should feel free to offer encouraging comments casually when you see teachers during the day. This will build rapport while signaling your investment in instructional leadership.

Daily rounds have several supervision pluses. They:

- Allow you to stay up-to-date on school-wide instruction. As you walk through classrooms, you observe what is taught. You also see teachers' instructional approaches and observe how students are learning. This information can be particularly useful when meeting with central office administrators, parent groups, or board members. When others ask questions or bring up issues, you will have the firsthand information you need to respond authoritatively. This will build their confidence in you as the school leader.
- Help you get to know your teachers' performance more thoroughly. When you see teachers over and over again, you cannot help but note instructional patterns. You will see their strengths and weaknesses. This information will be invaluable later during the teacher evaluation process.

- Permit you to fine-tune your perceptions of your faculty. Sometimes teachers earn reputations, both positive and negative, that they do not deserve. If your only classroom-based interaction with them is limited to required observations, you may never really get to know their true effectiveness. By increasing your classroom visitations, even if they are brief, you will form more accurate perceptions of your teachers.
- Help you identify potential teaching issues with newer faculty members before they become major problems. Have you ever had the experience of attending your parent organization meeting early in the year when suddenly a litany of concerns is raised about a particular new teacher? Through daily rounds, you will pick up on problems early so you can address them before others bring them to your attention.

Daily rounds are an invaluable tool you can use to establish a regular classroom presence. They also set the stage for more extensive supervision later. The more teachers feel comfortable with you in their classrooms, the greater the likelihood that you will see their normal day-to-day performance during teacher evaluation cycles. Also, you will see fewer "dog and pony" lessons if you are a regular classroom visitor.

DIRECTED SUPERVISION

While daily rounds are very informal and intended to increase visibility, directed supervision is more structured and purposeful. Although directive supervision is not as prescriptive as observations required as part of your district's teacher evaluation process, it can be useful in raising the supervision bar. To extend your supervision plan beyond daily rounds, consider building into your regular routine one or more of the four directed supervision techniques below.

- Student-focused walk-throughs
- District-wide walk-throughs
- Informal observations
- Mini-observations

Student-Focused Walk-Throughs

An emerging priority in classroom observation is a shift in observation focus from the teacher to the student. Administrators today place a priority on what and how students are learning. Under this approach, classroom walk-throughs center more on observing what students are doing and learning rather than teachers' actions.

Student-focused walk-throughs are similar to daily rounds but are longer and more purposeful. As such, if you are planning to conduct student-focused walk-throughs, you must ensure that teachers are not only aware that you will be dropping in but also the focus of the walk-throughs. This will help structure the experience while preparing teachers for discussion of the data gathered following the observations.

Moss and Brookhart (2013) suggest that principals and assistant principals avoid data collection checklists of teaching practices while targeting how students learn. They note that administrators can accomplish this by concentrating primarily on what students are doing, saying, writing, or making.

They suggest that administrators start by asking themselves three questions whenever they observe in classrooms. As they do, they should also record evidence of what they see.

- What did I see (Evidence of learning)?
- What does it mean (Evidence of what)?
- What do I need to learn more about (Gaps in my knowledge)?

They point out that administrators who want to increase the effectiveness of student-focused walk-throughs should "put themselves in students' shoes." To do so, they recommend that administrators ask themselves two additional questions.

- If I were a student in this classroom, what would I think was important for me to learn today, and how well would I believe I had to learn it?
- If I did everything the teacher asked me to do during the lesson, what would I actually learn, and what kind of evidence would I produce that I had learned?

Under this approach, administrators should interact with students whenever observing. This includes asking students questions about what they believe they are learning that day as well as how they will know if they have learned it. This level of observer/student interaction is a very effective way to gather information about instructional effectiveness. It also helps administrators hone their personal observation skills.

In addition, when employing this approach district-wide, administrators should be encouraged to meet with their administrative colleagues from other schools to discuss their observation experiences including data collected. The superintendent should also include formal discussions of these observations during district administrative team meetings. This additional administrative-level professional dialogue builds the supervision knowledge and skills of all administrators.

District Walk-Throughs

District walk-throughs are another directed supervision technique that can be a very effective way to gauge the implementation level of any district-wide instructional improvement initiative. In essence, they serve as implementation "integrity checks." For example, if improving the level of student engagement is a priority, this model will allow you to gather pertinent data quickly and efficiently. Similarly, if teachers are expected to implement a certain curriculum initiative, district walk-throughs can provide firsthand evidence.

District walk-throughs, though, are only effective when coupled with targeted professional development. Individual teachers and administrators must understand the latest research and best practices. You cannot expect improvement unless both teachers and administrators have a thorough understanding of the district instructional focus.

Once professional development is complete, an important next step is for both teachers and administrators to work together to define what its implementation looks like in the classroom. In addition, together they must also design the data collection methodology. These steps will enhance everyone's understanding of both the district-wide focus as well as performance expectations.

Once everyone is "on board," district administrators are ready to implement the process. How they approach district walk-throughs can vary based on local norms and the school's or district's culture. However, the most common approach is described below.

District administrative teams composed of members from the superintendent through building-level administrators and instructional coaches are assigned to gather data in a specific number of classrooms in a particular school. Some districts may also include teachers as observers. Generally, these walk-through observations range from ten to fifteen minutes per classroom.

Working as teams, they observe assigned teachers, then meet to process what they recorded. Data should be categorized school-wide rather than by individual teacher. What is unique about this process is that it shifts the focus from individual teacher evaluation to school and district effectiveness.

After each team completes its work, all teams should meet together to discuss and quantify raw data as well as to summarize their findings. Once this analysis is complete, sub-groups of team members should present their findings during individual school meetings. Each school faculty should be free to interpret data relative to implications for their school. Care should be taken to ensure that the presentation discusses district and/or school, not individual teacher, performance. During these sessions, faculty and administrators should be encouraged to engage in discussion and data analysis.

As the building administrator, you want to ensure that these presentations are not top-down summative assessments. Rather, the data should be used to encourage collaborative discussions. If done well, these meetings will enliven individual school professional conversations. They will also provide a useful gauge of how well the implementation of a district priority is progressing. Finally, the information is especially useful as a catalyst for more in-depth professional development.

District Walk-Through Advantages

For you as a building administrator, district walk-throughs offer several distinct pluses. They:

- Provide information upon which to build a school climate focused on instructional improvement;
- Allow you to gauge your faculty's investment in improvement;
- Create a process through which you reinforce district instructional priorities;
- Assist you in raising faculty understanding of research and best practice; and
- Reinforce your image in the school and district as an instructional partner with teachers.

Informal Classroom Observations

A third directive supervision technique is the informal classroom observation. These differ from the various walk-through models in that they have highly defined purposes, are longer in length, and require the supervisor to provide at least informal feedback to teachers.

Unlike district-required teacher evaluation observations, informal classroom observations do not include highly structured pre-observation or post-observation conferences. However, administrators are expected to meet with teachers informally before and after observations. Unless required by the district collective bargaining agreement or state mandates, administrators should not feel an expectation to prepare extensive written documentation. This flexibility makes informal observations more doable for busy administrators.

As with other supervision models previously discussed, administrators have latitude to select the observation process structure that best suits their individual situation. However, before deciding what approach to use, consider the following five factors.

Factor 1: Collective Bargaining Provisions

Before conducting any informal classroom observations, review your district's collective bargaining agreement. A sound approach is to discuss your observation plan with your superintendent before presenting it to teachers. You never want to exceed your authority. If you do, this will distract from your leadership, while creating distrust with teachers.

Factor 2: Purpose

Decide the primary purpose of the informal classroom observation. Is it primarily compliance or teacher development? What is important is that you as the supervisor establish a clear focus for your informal observations prior to designing the structure. Without specificity, your informal observation will be too generic and may be useless as a supervision tool. Discussed below are the two most common types of informal observation purposes.

Compliance. Under the compliance model, administrators target certain instructional or other supervision priorities to determine if teachers are complying with expectations. Examples of typical compliance expectations include:

- Posting daily lesson objectives prominently in the classroom;
- Beginning each class within thirty seconds of the start time;
- Maintaining an attractive classroom environment;
- Ensuring a high level of on-task student engagement; and
- Presenting a friendly, positive classroom demeanor.

The list of possible foci is unlimited. In all instances, though, a specific observation focus is essential.

Although the compliance approach may appear somewhat traditional, it has several advantages which should not be overlooked. First, there are times when you want to ensure consistency of performance among teachers. This does not happen by chance. As the school's leader, you must clearly communicate common expectations, which you reinforce through observation. For example, if one of your school's goals is for teachers to inform students what they will learn that day, this should be the observation focus. By following up through observation, you will reinforce this priority while demonstrating proactive supervision.

Another characteristic of the summative informal observation is that it allows you to observe how well teachers are implementing specific school or district priorities. As a supervisor, you will see firsthand whether teachers have truly internalized important concepts and skills learned during professional development. For example, consider the learning goals focus mentioned above. Teachers who say, "Here is what we're going to do today," rather than explain to students what they will learn demonstrate a lack of understanding. If you discover that teachers have not internalized some skill or concept, you will need to follow up with them.

Teacher Development. The second model focuses on teacher development. This differs from the compliance approach in that the supervisor's primary focus is on helping teachers grow as professionals.

Teacher development observations:

- Are tied directly to teaching and student learning;
- Are often structured around a simple data collection form;
- Generate classroom-based data about teaching performance and/or student learning; and
- Offer the potential to generate increased communication between the supervisor and teacher because they are based on collaborative discussions of teaching and learning in a nonjudgmental setting.

Factor 3: Length

As you design an informal observation plan, you should decide how much time to devote to each observation. The amount will vary and should be related directly to your purpose, whether it is compliance or teacher development. Rather than specifying an exact observation time-frame, observe only for as long as necessary to accomplish your purpose. However, most informal observations should be limited to twenty minutes or less.

Factor 4: Data Collection Method

For an informal observation to be effective, data collection is essential. Informal observations are not highly defined observation processes such as those required by district teacher evaluation plans. Yet, they require some structure. They should also be data driven. As a result, it is important to decide how and what data will be gathered.

Factor 5: Feedback

As you plan the informal observation process, you must decide how best to process the experience with teachers. This can be as simple as sharing informal comments in a conversational conference or by some more defined method you select. The key is ensuring that you always provide feedback.

INFORMAL OBSERVATION ADVANTAGES

Informal observations can enhance your overall supervision effectiveness in several ways. They:

- Limit the amount of paperwork document completion and the number of mandatory meetings required for more formal observation cycles. Because they are less time consuming, you can increase the number of times you observe teachers every year.

- Allow you to improve your communication with teachers especially since these observations are not directly linked to the formal teacher evaluation process. Rather than "writing up" what you observed, you and the teacher are free to discuss each other's perspectives. Such a less-threatening setting facilitates greater communication.

- Identify instructional issues, curriculum deficiencies, or student-related problems that might be missed if you observed teachers only once or twice a year. However, if the deficiency is substantial enough to warrant more direct action, you should follow through quickly.

- Help you become a more informed leader. The more you are in classrooms, the more exposure you have to daily instruction. As a result, you will become a more knowledgeable and skilled supervisor.

Mini-Observations

In addition to various informal observations models, mini-observation is one other supervisory technique that is growing in popularity. In fact, some school districts may require them as a component of the district's teacher evaluation process. Mini-observations differ from informal observations because they have increased structure and focus.

Mini-observations are also especially useful in setting the stage for future observations. They allow you to enter the formal teacher evaluation process with an increased understanding of teachers' strengths and potential areas for improvement. Rather than using the first regular classroom observation to establish this baseline, you can use the mini-observation to accomplish this.

As with other supervision techniques, no one mini-observation method is preferred. Although most approaches are district or school-based, Marshall's prescriptive mini-observation framework warrants consideration. His administrative-driven approach is grounded in six questions. He recommends that one or more of the following questions serve as the basis for a mini-observation (Marshall, 2012).

- Are there any physical safety concerns?
- Is the classroom environment psychologically safe?
- What is the lesson objective?
- How effective is the teacher's instruction?
- Are students actively engaged in the learning?
- Is there evidence of student assessment?

To conduct any effective mini-observation, you should think specifics. Rather than just noting general perceptions, you must record specific details. For example, if you are concerned about the psychological safety of students, you would point out exactly what the teacher said or did to validate students. Simply stating that the classroom environment made each student feel safe is of no value.

Also, only offering broad complimentary feedback is useless. Teachers see this type of supervision as meaningless. On the other hand, teachers will react positively to comments that are concrete and helpful.

Too often, administrators avoid providing teachers with concrete feedback either because they are not well prepared or because they want to avoid any supervision discomfort. What they fail to recognize is that teachers view this type of supervision as irrelevant. To earn the respect of teachers and be a more effective supervisor, you need to provide feedback that is concrete, constructive, and specific.

If you develop your own your mini-observation framework, here are four steps to follow, which will help you implement a sound process.

Step 1: Work with your faculty members to clarify the focus of any mini-observations. By engaging teachers in this discussion, you enhance everyone's understanding of best practice including yours.

Step 2: Identify together examples of what constitutes exceptional performance. It is one thing to talk about specific teaching or learning indicators on a theoretical level. It is quite another to develop a list of exemplars. The more concrete and visual the examples of top level performance are, the greater the likelihood that both you and your teachers will understand performance expectations.

Step 3: Build in opportunities for teachers to share their perspectives with colleagues. An effective way to accomplish this is to encourage teachers to lead discussions of mini-observation focuses during faculty meetings. If you are able to create such a teacher leadership environment in your school, you will raise the supervision bar for the faculty as a whole. Also, you will experience increased faculty buy-in.

Step 4: Make classroom visitations a preplanned (not surprise) event. Mini-observations are not designed as drop-in visits, but rather as an extension of professional development. If teachers know when you will be visiting their classrooms, they will be much better prepared. You will also see their best performance. In a subtle way, you will be encouraging them to "stretch" naturally.

Directed supervision, including student-focused walk-throughs, district walk-throughs, informal observations, and mini-observations, should be essential components of your overall supervision plan. By placing a high priority on such activities, you can significantly increase your effectiveness as a supervisor. You will also expand the professional knowledge of teaching and learning for both you and your faculty.

POINTS TO REMEMBER

If you hope to have a significant impact on your school's culture, teacher performance, and, ultimately, student learning, you must raise the supervision bar. To do so, provide decisive leadership while placing a priority on relationship building. Also, remember that visibility is an important element of supervision success. By building in such techniques as daily rounds, classroom walk-throughs, and directive supervision, you will earn the respect of all stakeholders while truly making a difference in student achievement.

SIX

Evaluating for Excellence

In addition to supervising teachers, another important responsibility of school leaders is teacher evaluation. Marzano (2012) identified a useful framework that defines the two important purposes of teacher evaluation: developing and measuring teachers. He notes that addressing both is essential if you hope to hire, develop, and retain truly strong faculty members. You cannot focus exclusively on development or you will never discriminate between teachers who are outstanding performers and those who should be dismissed. On the other hand, you cannot expect to encourage teachers to grow as professionals if your evaluation method is merely judgmental.

For years, the primary focus of teacher evaluation was essentially on the development side. Because of teacher tenure job protection rights, administrators often placed minimal emphasis on performance accountability. Recently national calls for more effective teacher evaluation have begun to shift the focus toward the judgmental/summative purpose of teacher evaluation. More than ever, political leaders, parents, and even the general public are much less willing to accept or ignore what they perceive as poor teaching. This shift has changed the way administrators must look at the teacher evaluation process.

THE CRACK IN THE TENURE SHIELD

Until very recently, most public school teachers across the country benefited from teacher tenure laws or collective bargaining provisions, which made the dismissal of tenured teachers extremely difficult. Only in cases of egregious behavior was the dismissal of tenured teachers reasonably doable. Teacher tenure was defined in state law and sometimes protected by state constitutional provisions. These laws set a high threshold for dismissing poor teachers and complicated procedures to implement the process. Complicating the process further were teacher unions, which negotiated contractual rights. Through powerful lobbying, unions vigorously protected tenure. As a result, administrators faced daunting odds if they chose to dismiss even poor teachers.

Over the years, parents and school boards had become accustomed to the intractability of tenure. Parents often accepted poor teacher performance because they believed that tenure laws made teacher dismissal nearly impossible. Administrators contributed to this culture of complacency by taking dismissal off the teacher evaluation table. As a consequence, below average or even unsatisfactory teachers often continued their careers until they chose to leave.

Teachers perceived job security more as a right than a privilege. In some school districts, principals who questioned teachers' performance were often met with school-wide faculty resistance. In fact, some principals who evaluated faculty members as less than excellent found their own leadership questioned, even by their superintendents and school board members. These realities raise the question: How did this job protective culture ever develop in public education?

HISTORICAL BACKGROUND OF TEACHER TENURE

From the founding of the United States, local politics have played a role in employment and dismissal of public employees, including teachers. Political leaders often used the employment process to reward friends and supporters or to punish opponents. Until relatively recently, this patronage system has been an accepted practice throughout the nation (Kersten, 2006).

As patronage system abuses began to mount in the late nineteenth century, increased public dissatisfaction emerged, which raised patronage to a national discussion level. This dialogue culminated with the passage of the Pendleton Civil Service Reform Act in 1883. Under the leadership of Ohio senator George Pendleton and the National Service League, federal legislation was passed that created the civil service system. Under this law, employers were required to hire and retain employees on the basis of merit, not political favoritism (Huvaere, 1997).

Although this legislation did not apply directly to public school employees, it fueled a debate on job security and patronage practices in public education. Contributing to this national debate was the National Education Association (NEA), which in 1885 called for similar protections for teachers. By 1886, the NEA formed the Committee on Salaries, Tenure, and Pensions whose focus was to advocate for similar protections for teachers (Huvaere, 1997).

As political support for teacher employment protections grew, New Jersey became the first state to pass a teacher tenure law in 1909 (Educational Commission of the States, 1999). For the first time, teachers received legal due process employment protection rights.

Proponents of this legislation argued that it would improve the quality of education in New Jersey. Interestingly, some of the very points made to support passage of these tenure laws are now the ones used to call for its abolition. New Jersey tenure supporters said the law would:

- Attract more qualified teachers. By offering increased job security, the best teachers would more likely choose to teach in New Jersey than in neighboring states, which did not provide tenure protection.
- Increase the efficiency of the school district through the improved teacher retention.
- Make teaching as a profession a more attractive career option by providing teachers with increased political and economic security.
- Eliminate favoritism in hiring and dismissal.

While other states lagged behind New Jersey's lead, by the mid-1940s, approximately 70 percent of teachers in the United States were protected by some form of tenure (National Education Association Alaska, 2005). By the end of the twentieth century, nearly every state and the District of Columbia offered teacher employment protection through tenure laws or negotiated collective bargaining (Educational Commission of the States, 1999).

Once passed, state teacher tenure laws remained sacrosanct in state legislatures for decades. Only in the early 2000s did shifting political tides truly change the course of unbending support for teacher tenure. As reports of poor educational performance mounted and it became politically popular to challenge the quality of teaching, general public support for education including strong teacher tenure protection began to wane. States such as Colorado, New Mexico, South Dakota, and Florida eliminated tenure, while Oklahoma tightened due process timelines. Other states such as Michigan and Connecticut streamlined due process provisions, while Wisconsin made tenure policies a function of local collective bargaining (Frey, 2010).

This trend of modifying teacher tenure rules and regulations is poised to grow rather than diminish. As a result, you need to ensure that you are up-to-date on your state teacher evaluation legal requirements. You must also be prepared to respond to the growing focus on measuring teacher performance. Finally, you must be ready to respond to stakeholders who will expect you either to help teachers improve their performance or dismiss them.

Given these emerging changes in policies, legal requirements, and public perception, a key question is: How can you best evaluate teachers for excellence especially as the purpose has shifted to a more judgmental focus?

DIFFERENTIATED EVALUATION

In the past, nontenured and tenured teachers were usually evaluated using a very similar process. The most significant difference was generally the frequency of classroom observations rather than the method itself. Nontenured teachers were typically observed more often than their tenured colleagues.

Today, more and more, administrators are expected to differentiate their supervisory and evaluation methods to accommodate individual teacher needs. Factors such as whether faculty members are tenured or not, their years of experience, and their day-to-day performance levels should all affect the scope and depth of the how administrators evaluate each teacher.

Experienced administrators know that their teachers perform at a wide variety of levels. To appreciate this point, ask yourself if you have any two teachers who perform at exactly the same level? You may have some with similar performance levels; however, most likely, the performance of individual teachers varies a great deal. In fact, you probably have some beginning teachers who perform like seasoned veterans. At the same time, you likely work with experienced teachers who perform comparably to novices.

Because of these performance variances, a key to improving teacher evaluation is differentiating how you supervise them and varying your evaluation methods to meet individual teacher needs. One way to accomplish this is to begin by categorizing each of your teachers on a performance continuum from master teacher to poor performer.

Master teachers are the individuals who are your star performers. When you observe them in their classrooms, work with them on committees, or see them interact with others, you are hard pressed to offer any improvement suggestions. These are the types of individuals that all administrators wish they could clone.

At the opposite end of the continuum are your poorest performers. They are not only ineffective in the classroom but in every other aspect of performance. They appear unmotivated and have difficulty relating to children. They use students, parents, and administrators as scapegoats for poor performance and can have a poisonous effect on the school culture. When you evaluate them, you struggle to narrow the list of improvement suggestions to a manageable number of items.

Most school districts have very few performers at either end of this spectrum. Many more teachers fall somewhere in-between. Given these realities, to be a highly effective evaluator, you must get to know each of your teachers well enough to place them at the appropriate spot on the performance continuum from poor performer to master teacher. Once you do, you will be better prepared to differentiate your evaluation process to fit their individual needs.

As an evaluator, you ideally have some autonomy to customize your teacher evaluation process as you see fit. In reality, though, you will likely be restricted by collective bargaining provisions, state requirements, a prescribed teacher evaluation rubric, or years of district and school cultural expectations. Nonetheless, the more you can differentiate your evaluation process to include specific supervision techniques targeted at individual teacher performance levels, the more effective you will be as an evaluator.

To initiate the differentiation process, begin by categorizing your teachers into one of two groups: beginners and veterans. You will be expected to approach novice teachers differently from veterans. This is because the primary focus of new teacher evaluation is making a decision about reemployment.

Evaluating Beginning Teachers

Although job protection rights are no longer available in some states, they are still a reality in most. Therefore, whether or not your state has some form of tenure or legal due process rights, you must view the first one to three years of teaching as a true probation period. You must decide whether you will reemploy these teachers during their probationary years and ultimately recommend them for tenure.

This is a very judgmental process. During the first year or two of employment, you have the greatest latitude to make continued employment decisions. After that, you run the risk of complicating the dismissal of a novice or nontenured teacher. Remember that even in states without tenure protections, the dismissal of teachers early in their careers, who have established relationships with staff members, students, and parents, can be quite complex and, at times, political. As a result, you should make tough judgment calls before relationship issues become a major factor.

How you approach the teacher evaluation process with beginning faculty members can make all the difference in your effectiveness. Here are several strategies to consider that will help you optimize your effectiveness as an evaluator of beginning teachers.

Strategy 1: Evaluate teachers based on their overall performance. Have you ever heard administrators tell you that they reemployed certain beginning teachers because they were excellent with students even though they were difficult employees? In the next breath, some probably admit that they wished they had not. Teachers often equate good performance only with how they perform in the classroom. The truth is that excellent performance is not limited to classroom instruction. To build a strong, collaborative faculty, you need teachers who perform well in the classroom. Just as important, they must be good faculty members who relate well with children and parents as well as colleagues and administrators (Kersten, 2010).

Strategy 2: Do not hesitate to identify areas for improvement.   Although it is important to be a positive evaluator, being too complimentary with beginning teachers sends the wrong message. All new teachers with potential for excellence recognize that they have room for growth as professionals. They expect that their evaluators will point out areas for improvement.

Too often administrators err on the side of emphasizing the positive while minimizing comments about improvement. A better approach is to evaluate teachers by being direct, fair, objective, professional, and judgmental. As part of this, you must make sure that you support your assessment with specific evidence. If you do not, these impressionable novices will lose respect for the evaluation process and possibly you as their evaluator.

Strategy 3: Balance compliments with constructive criticism.   New teachers are nervous. Even those who project a great deal of confidence actually worry about their success. Do you remember how you felt the first time your evaluator entered your classroom? Chances are that your new teachers feel the same way.

By the time you begin the summative evaluation cycle, beginning teachers have already entered the anticipation stage of their development. They are anxious about their success and worry about reemployment. They are facing the realities of teaching head on. During this developmental phase, you must find a balance between encouraging them and offering constructive criticism. Different teachers and situations require varied doses of each.

Strategy 4: Differentiate between poor performers and those with potential.   One of the very first evaluative judgments you must make is determining if a novice teacher has the potential to succeed. One effective way to do so is to build supervisory techniques such as daily rounds, classroom walk-throughs, and informal observations into your pre-evaluation routine. These tools can help you identify teachers who lack the requisite personal, professional, and/or pedagogical skills you desire. Your initial perceptions can then be tested through the evaluation process. By employing these approaches, you will be positioned to determine who truly has potential and who should be dismissed.

Strategy 5: Recognize the difference between what can truly be improved and what cannot.   All beginning teachers have areas for improvement. The issue is whether an individual's weaknesses can actually be improved through evaluation and experience. Successful administrators will tell you that most new teachers can develop their knowledge of teaching and learning. What are nearly impossible to change are a person's disposition, personality, and outlook on life. An unhappy, negative personality is not fixable. New teachers may be able to mask their true personality for some time. However, ultimately it will emerge.

On the other hand, some novices may not have fully learned the latest teaching methods, participated in curriculum development, or dealt with challenging classroom management issues. These individuals may only need time to develop their knowledge and skills. As the evaluator, your responsibility is to decide if they have true growth potential. There is no magic formula to make this determination. Furthermore, you will never be correct one hundred percent of the time. However, if you employ a variety of supervision techniques, complete the teacher evaluation process, and tap your personal judgment, you will increase your chances of making the correct long-term decision.

Strategy 6: Be a decisive decision-maker. By nature, those who aspire to careers in education tend to be pleasers. Their natural tendency is to be positive and supportive. They see themselves more as helpers than critics. As a result, some administrators struggle with delivering criticism or informing teachers that their contracts will not be renewed. Most would rather give even the most marginal performers another opportunity to show improvement rather than dismiss them.

To improve your school and maximize student learning, you must overcome the tendency to be overly positive. This means that you must be a decisive decision-maker who is unafraid to dismiss a novice teacher who does not show potential for high performance.

On the surface, this may seem especially unfair, especially in states where second year reemployment decisions must be made as early as March. In some instances, beginning teachers may only have until December to demonstrate performance potential. By then, reemployment decisions are probably already made. Superintendents often alert their boards of education about potential nonrenewals early to avoid surprising boards a few months later. While the timeframe is short and administrators may lack some data, it is also unfair to foist questionable teachers on students for years to come.

If you reemploy beginning teachers with whom you have concerns, you open yourself up to protracted problems. Some states, such as Illinois, gradually increase procedural and legal dismissal requirements for beginning teachers each of the first few years they are employed. Waiting longer to make dismissal decisions requires administrators to meet additional requirements.

Another potential problem you can face is politics. The longer marginal teachers are employed, the more these individuals ensconce themselves in the school's culture. Groups of teachers, students, and parents are never privy to all the teacher performance information you are. As a result, they may judge a teacher's performance exclusively through their personal interactions. Consequently, if you decide to dismiss the teacher who is well liked, your motives may be questioned. They may even fight the dismissal publicly. Remember, it is in your best interest to make the employment decision as early as possible, most often during the first year of employment.

Evaluating Experienced Teachers

Any one-size-fits-all model of teacher evaluation is quickly becoming obsolete, particularly for experienced teachers. As public expectations for teachers to demonstrate measurable performance grows, administrators are expected to accurately document teacher performance. The simple checklist models and broad narratives of the past are no longer adequate. Evaluators must do more than visit classrooms and provide teachers with generic feedback. They must zero in on research-based instructional practices that lead to increased student learning.

The emergence of standards-driven teacher evaluation models as popularized by Charlotte Danielson and Robert Marzano have reshaped the evaluation landscape. Evaluators today must have a much deeper understanding of research-based teaching practices. They must develop the tools necessary to document teacher performance as objectively as possible based on researched-based practices.

Developing Your Personal Knowledge Base

One of the great challenges current administrators face is in becoming an expert in researched-based teaching practices. Another is developing the skills needed to apply what they learned to practice. Most experienced administrators generally first learned how to evaluate teachers based on how they were evaluated themselves. Newer graduates may have been exposed to research-based models but only at cursory level during their preparation programs.

Even today, most veteran and novice administrators alike evaluate teachers with limited knowledge of the latest information available. One of these is the Common Core Standards. To truly evaluate for excellence, you must place a priority on your personal professional development to become a truly knowledgeable, skilled evaluator. To do so, ask yourself the following question: How can I develop the knowledge of research-based teaching practices necessary to be a very effective teacher evaluator?

As you consider this question, think for a moment how many people learn to play tennis. A common approach is to gather a group of friends, buy some racquets and balls, and head to the local courts. Once there, they try to hit balls back and forth. Since they have seen tennis on television and may have swung a racquet at some point in their childhood, they think learning the game will be relatively easy. They do not invest in lessons. Rather, they rely on how they see others play and try to emulate what they do.

Unfortunately, under this approach, they probably spend more time chasing balls or practicing poor technique than learning the game. Yes, they are playing but not as effectively as they could with proper instruction and focused practice. Within a short period of time, most probably decide that tennis is just too difficult and quit the game.

Administrators often develop their evaluation styles and practices in a similar manner. One difference though is that poor tennis players can just quit without any consequences. Administrators are not in this position. Because teacher evaluation is an integral part of their responsibilities, they must continue to evaluate their teachers even if what they do is minimally effective. The results of their evaluations, though, will have a significant impact on the lives of hundreds and even thousands of students.

To become a highly effective evaluator, you must commit to ramping up your professional knowledge base. If you do not, you will be underprepared to implement a standards-based teacher evaluation process. Administrative experience alone will not be enough. You must seek out opportunities to grow your understanding of what teachers do to make a real difference in student learning, in addition to examining the plethora of supervision strategies available today.

Here are several suggestions on ways to accomplish this.

- Actively participate in district staff development programs, especially those targeting instruction and student achievement. Too often administrators see professional development as something teachers do rather than as an opportunity for their own professional development. They either focus on other administrative tasks during this time or participate passively. A better approach is to immerse yourself in the activities as fully as you expect teachers to do. Not only will you learn a great deal, but you will benefit from reflective discussions with teachers.

- Seek out workshops or conferences that address the connection between instruction and student achievement as well as supervision strategies. These typically feature presenters who are leaders in the field. Target your attendance at sessions which offer the most potential for learning. This time will prove invaluable to you as your school's instructional leader.

- Look for opportunities to participate in your district's instructional rounds. If you do not have this program available in your district, consider discussing beginning one with your superintendent. They are usually open to creative professional development suggestions from their administrators.

- Initiate book talk groups both with teachers in your school and administrative colleagues. Focus them on the latest best practices in teaching, student learning research, and assessment methods. Often teachers and administrators are too day-to-day focused to even consider book talks. However, as the school's leader, you are in a position to influence others. Book talks offer great potential to engage colleagues in reflective professional conversations.

Implementing a Dynamic Evaluation Approach

Once you have built a solid knowledge base and committed yourself to ongoing improvement, you are prepared to evaluate for excellence. However, effective evaluation is more than just understanding what highly effective teachers do. You must become adept at applying what you know during actual teacher evaluation cycles.

To more fully appreciate this, consider the following question. Have you ever had college professors who were highly regarded as experts in their fields but could not teach? They may have known a great deal about their program areas but not how to instruct others. Similar to such professors, some administrators can articulately discuss the latest research but do not understand how to translate what they know into effective teacher evaluation practice. Two administrators could evaluate the same teacher with very different results. One might be a much more effective evaluator than the other.

A classic example of this occurred during the implementation of the clinical supervision model during the 1980s. Administrator after administrator attended workshops, read materials, and participated in clinical supervision training. Yet, how they implemented what they learned varied dramatically. Some interpreted the process as a rigid formula. They regularly employed the pre-observation conference, classroom observation, and post-observation conference during their evaluation cycles but provided meaningless feedback to teachers. They completed the steps but lost the gestalt. In contrast, other more successful evaluators saw it as a dynamic tool, which could be individualized to meet each teacher's needs.

As mentioned earlier, teacher evaluation is a dynamic process. The most effective teacher evaluators understand how to modify and apply their district teacher evaluation process to meet individual teacher performance needs. They do much more than talk about teaching research. They apply what they know during day-to-day supervision and evaluation.

It is here where the art of supervision becomes critical. There is no secret formula to guarantee evaluation success. There is no one approach which, when replicated, is more effective than another. Your evaluation success is tied to how well you apply everything you know about effective teaching, supervision, and evaluation as you evaluate teachers.

Chapter 4 presented a plethora of supervision approaches that you can incorporate into each teacher's annual evaluation cycle as appropriate. However, simply using them rigidly without customizing them to the unique needs of your teachers will have little if any impact on their performance. To be the most effective evaluator you can be, you must view the teacher evaluation process as dynamic, not stagnant. This means that you must consider each teacher's position on the performance continuum as you decide how to best evaluate him or her.

To help you individualize the process for each teacher, consider the following strategies.

Strategy 1: Recognize that your teachers perform across a broad spectrum of effectiveness. The reason generic evaluation processes are ineffective is that they are static rather than dynamic. Evaluators focus too much on the process itself. They are most concerned about completing each step and meeting all deadlines. They consider successful evaluation as simply completing all required steps in the process. They do not see it as a tool that heavily impacts teacher performance.

To become a highly effective evaluator, you must approach teacher evaluation from a different perspective. Yes, you must complete all required steps of the district teacher evaluation process. However, you must remember that these steps are only the structural part of evaluation. What are most important are selecting appropriate supervision strategies and using them to impact teacher professional development.

Teachers' performance in most schools ranges from poor to highly skilled. This means that you must tailor both the approaches you use and how you use them as closely as possible to the needs of each teacher. To do so, consider the following questions as part of your planning process for each teacher's evaluation cycle.

- Where would you rank the teacher on the continuum from master teacher to poor performer?
- Does the teacher have self-awareness of his/her performance level?
- How capable is the teacher of accepting constructive criticism?
- Have you seen positive improvements in the teacher's performance in the past when suggestions were offered?
- Have you seen this teacher growing as a professional over the years?
- What personal traits does the teacher have that indicate how open he or she is to improvement?
- Is the teacher generally responsive to ideas or more passive-aggressive?
- Does the teacher demonstrate initiative in everyday performance?

This list is far from comprehensive. However, it reflects the type and scope of pre-evaluation assessment you will need to complete before you determine how best to tailor each evaluation.

Strategy 2: Deal with rather than ignore extremely poor tenured teacher performance.   As personally challenging as it can be to honestly evaluate poor tenured teachers, you cannot ignore or minimize them. This means that you must focus almost exclusively on summative evaluation. You must let them know early in the school year through your words and actions that they are performing well below district expectations. You do not want them to be surprised later.

You should ensure that you use supervision techniques that lay the groundwork for a more summative focus. Rather than offering too much encouragement, provide feedback that is both concrete and direct. You need to let them know that you have concerns about their performance.

Besides offering verbal feedback, another way to show your concern is to increase the number and depth of supervision-related interactions. This may mean increasing the frequency of informal walk-throughs and informal observations while providing written comments following each. This is very time consuming but essential. However, if you are nondirective or fail to document what you observe at least through emails, these poor performers will not feel pressured to improve. You also will not have adequately documented evidence to dismiss them.

For some teachers, elevated supervision may kick-start their performance. They may never have felt the need to improve previously. At first, this may even create some discomfort with other faculty members. However, once you apply this more direct approach with ineffective teachers, others will recognize that you have raised your performance expectations.

For others, the direct approach may have the opposite effect. By documenting their performance, they may even regress. Ultimately, this may mean recommending dismissal if this option is feasible in your state. Before walking down this path, make sure you have discussed what you plan to do with your superintendent and/or other central office administrators. Their support and guidance, including any legal implications, will be critical as you increase expectations for your very poor performing teachers.

Strategy 3: Focus on specific not generalities.   Highly effective, differentiated supervision and evaluation require specific not general teacher feedback that is grounded in the latest research. Providing only generic comments or focusing feedback on nonresearch-based information, particularly with veteran teachers, only weakens your position as an evaluator. These teachers will not take you seriously as an evaluator. Also, your superintendent and possibly school board members might question your thoroughness.

To be the most effective evaluator you can be, tie all supervision and evaluation feedback directly to performance indicators that are linked to research-based teaching practices. Just as important, make sure that your feedback also ties to performance indicators in your district's teacher evaluation plan. This is especially critical if you need to place a teacher on a remediation plan or even move toward dismissal. Such an approach clearly delineates areas of concerns for evaluated teachers. It also demonstrates that your evaluation was based directly on observable, documented, research-based performance indicators.

Strategy 4: Show flexibility with your highest performing teachers. School district teacher evaluation plans generally require evaluators to adhere to the same basic procedures for all veteran teachers. For example, you may be expected to complete two or three observation cycles annually for all teachers regardless of performance level. The most effective evaluators meet this requirement but alter how they interact with their highest performing teachers. Some may encourage these teachers to lead the evaluation process, while others may treat each phase as a collegial conversation. Still others may offer only the required summative ratings while encouraging teachers to focus on their personal professional development needs.

To make your teacher evaluation process useful for your highest performing teachers, you must clearly differentiate it as much as possible from that of other teachers. Do not be afraid to invite the most competent teachers to suggest what they believe would be most helpful to them. Then, find ways to either modify what is currently required or add activities or steps as necessary. You should do everything you can to avoid going through the teacher evaluation process motions, which will leave both you and the teachers feeling professionally unsatisfied.

Committing to Ethical Evaluation

Finally, you must also recognize that no matter how diligently you adhere to mandated teacher evaluation requirements, your evaluations will never be 100 percent objective. Because of the inherent subjectivity of any evaluation system, it is important to commit to being a highly ethical evaluator. This means reporting what you observed as accurately as possible and not manipulating teacher performance data or exaggerating any areas for improvement. If you do not, teachers will lose respect for you and the evaluation process. You will also develop a reputation as an arbitrary and capricious evaluator. This could ultimately undermine your leadership. It may even drive teachers to challenge your performance at the central office or board levels.

Evaluating veteran teachers is challenging, particularly since it is part science and part art. If you prepare yourself well, understand how to tailor evaluation to the unique needs of each teacher, and unabashedly take a strong leadership role, you can make a real difference in teaching and learning in your school.

POINTS TO REMEMBER

Teacher evaluation has two distinct purposes: developing and measuring teachers. Each is essential to any comprehensive teacher evaluation plan. However, the summative evaluation component has grown in importance with the weakening of teacher job protections nationally and greater expectations for student performance. Administrators today are expected more than ever to either help teachers improve or dismiss them.

Much of your success as an evaluator depends on your knowledge of research-based teaching practices and the plethora of supervision options available to you. Before beginning your annual teacher evaluations, focus on ensuring that you are well prepared in these areas. You cannot be a well-respected evaluator without knowing what it is that teachers can do that makes them effective.

Once you have ramped up your own professional development, you must recognize that teacher evaluation is a dynamic, not static, process. Since no one-size-fits-all supervision or evaluation model exists, you must differentiate each to respond to the individual developmental needs of your teachers.

For beginning teachers this means that you must focus on whether you will reemploy them. For veterans, you must meet district evaluation process requirements but also individualize your approach to their personal performance levels. For below average teachers, this may mean evaluating them as you would any novice teacher. For your most talented, you must find ways to modify your interactions with them throughout the process. You want to make sure that the process has value for them. You may also need to add activities or steps to the process, which will emanate from collegial conversations including teachers' self-analyses. If you do, you will make a real difference in teaching and learning in your school.

SEVEN

Functioning as a Collaborative Administrative Team Member

Building-level administrators, by the nature of their positions, tend to be primarily school-focused. They see their success directly linked to how well they manage their schools and the quality of educational programs and services they offer. These, of course, are important responsibilities. However, the most successful principals also understand that they do not operate in a vacuum. Rather, they see themselves as integral members of the district administrative team, not as independent contractors. They understand that true leadership extends beyond the school doors.

Within this context, principals value the synergy that results from being a fully functioning member of the school district administrative team. They understand that much more can be accomplished at both the district and building levels if all members of the administrative staff work together collaboratively. They know that distancing themselves from other district administrators limits their long-term effectiveness and even brings into question their leadership effectiveness.

Building a district administrative team does not happen by chance. It must be created and fostered over time. Although the primary responsibility for its development rests with the superintendent, building-level administrators play a vital role too. What they choose to support or not support will directly impact the efficacy of the school district's administrative team and ultimately the success of the school.

Although administrative teamwork is important for all-school district functions, it is especially essential when hiring, supervising, and evaluating teachers. A strong, well-functioning district administrative team will enhance the effectiveness of each of these very important administrative responsibilities.

Unfortunately, some administrators fail to recognize the importance of teamwork. Rather than looking for opportunities to contribute to the district administrative team, they become almost exclusively school focused. Others promote themselves at the expense of their colleagues. In either instance, they consciously or unconsciously act in ways that create stumbling blocks to teamwork. Discussed below are ways that building-level administrators who are not collaborative undermine district efforts to build a cohesive administrative team.

Being unsupportive of district administrative decisions. In any school district, there will be times when the superintendent must make unpopular decisions. The most successful superintendents do so only after completing extensive "homework." They also invite their administrative team members to provide any and all perspectives. Such an approach increases the likelihood of the superintendent making informed decisions and avoiding unanticipated problems. However, once a decision is made, all administrators are expected to support it.

A timely example of an issue that will impact personnel is a growing school district budget deficit. Experienced superintendents know that they must act promptly to reduce expenditures. Otherwise, the district's situation could become dire, which would create potential political chaos. Most of the time, the only viable option to improve the district's financial position is to reduce personnel expenditures.

In this example, after carefully reviewing all options, your superintendent concludes that the district must limit all new hires' service credit to no more than one year. Personally, you believe that such a low level will restrict the quality of faculty members you can hire. You also know that parents and teachers will be very unhappy with this hiring cap and partially blame you for the change. You now have a decision to make. Will you publicly support the limit even though you may not agree with it? Or, will you tell teachers and parents that you have to implement it because you were directed to by your superintendent?

As you weigh your response, you recognize that if you support this controversial decision, you may lose some support in your school. At the same time, how you respond to this situation will show whether you are truly a team player. Dilemmas such as these are inherent elements of school leadership. To be viewed as a team player, you must align yourself fully with district central office administrators no matter how personally stressful this position may be.

A sure way to lose the support of your superintendent and other district administrators is to be publicly nonsupportive or even neutral. Some administrators try to deflect criticism from themselves for an unpopular decision. They tell others that a decision was made by the superintendent and that they were required to enforce it. Rather than supporting their administrative colleagues, they look to separate themselves from the decision. Although this may initially minimize some personal criticism, it will erode trust with administrative team members. Remember that being a team member means fully supporting any administrative decisions once they are made even if you have spoken against them during administrative team meetings.

Failing to be inclusive. Some of the worst personnel decisions principals make are those that are hasty. Because they feel pressured by time consuming day-to-day job responsibilities, principals are more susceptible to overly quick decision-making. Rather than taking the time needed to consider something thoroughly, they react. At other times, poor decisions result not from work pressures but from overconfidence or even arrogance. In either case, these administrators tend to make personnel decisions independently rather than by involving their district administrative team members. By failing to consult with their administrative colleagues, they miss an important opportunity to benefit from their expertise. They can also damage their working relationships with these important team members.

One area in which administrative teamwork can be especially useful is during the teacher hiring process. Principals who choose not to invite other administrative team members into their selection process decrease the likelihood that they will hire the strongest teachers. They rely purely on their own judgment rather than ensuring that they have considered multiple perspectives. To increase both the scope and depth of your teacher selection process, make sure you have done your due diligence. Also, include your district administrative team members as much as possible.

Developing alliances with certain district administrators. For district administrators to work collaboratively as a team, each must be committed to the team concept. If any administrators are excluded, the efficacy of the administrative team is compromised. In some school districts, it is common for sub-groups of administrators to meet outside of the full team. They actively discuss topics, create alliances, and plan their responses as a unit rather than as individuals. For example, the district's elementary principals may form an alliance that includes both social and professional activities while excluding central office or even secondary school administrators.

Such alliances undermine the effectiveness of the district administrative team. They create "camps of administrators" as well as make some administrators feel like outsiders rather than valued team members. Left unchecked, they slowly erode the effectiveness of the broader team and lead to animosity among administrators. They also make it very difficult for district administrators to work together as a team on hiring, supervising, and evaluating teachers.

TEAM BUILDING STRATEGIES

Recognizing and avoiding administrative missteps that undermine the development of a highly effective district administrative team are important. At the same time, understanding what you can do to foster administrative team building in your district is even more important. As your school's leader, you must place a personal priority on building the best possible relationships you can with administrators in your school district. Remember that you can accomplish a great deal more when you work with rather than without their assistance.

This point though raises an important question for you to consider. What can you do to contribute to the development of a highly effective district administrative team? Discussed below are strategies available that will demonstrate your commitment to being a positive, productive district administrative team member. Recognize though that the size of your school district will require you to adjust how you might make use of some these strategies.

Strategy 1: Be inclusive.   Over your career, you have probably worked with teaching staffs composed of faculty with very diverse personalities and perspectives. They were probably hired over several decades by a variety of administrators who, too, were very different. A similar level of diversity usually exists within the school district administrative ranks and may include contrasting leadership styles. These differences can interfere with administrative team building as certain administrators naturally gravitate to each other, sometimes at the exclusion of others.

Yet some districts develop cohesive administrative teams even with such diversity. Often the difference is a commitment from key administrators to work together as a team while accepting personality and leadership style variances.

How do they do this? They make a point of treating others as equals. They are careful not to disenfranchise some administrators at the expense of others. When discussing topics such as teacher evaluation at their district administrative team meetings, they engage each member rather than steering the conversation to a selected few. When planning social administrative outings, they make sure to include everyone.

Such actions demonstrate inclusiveness. They let others know that they are valued members of the team while encouraging full participation from everyone. If you approach your colleagues from an inclusive rather than competitive or self-focused perspective, other administrators, especially those from the central office, will view you as a team player.

Strategy 2: Make a point of touching base with each of your colleagues on a regular basis.   As was discussed earlier, it is very easy to become school-bound. However, the hiring, supervision, and evaluation processes provide you with many natural opportunities to reach out to your colleagues. You cannot wait until someone else calls you. You should take the initiative. Although at first you may feel that you are the only one doing so, in the end your actions will pay dividends for you and the team.

To begin, make phone calls to other principals or even drop in to visit with your superintendent or assistant superintendents. To appreciate the power of a mere call or visit, consider how you might feel if one of your colleagues reached out to you? Such informal interactions will strengthen individual administrative colleague relationships while generating productive professional dialogue. They can also be catalysts for other administrators to follow your lead.

Focusing on issues or questions you might have about hiring or teacher evaluation when you reach out can open the communication door. For example, if you are a relatively new district administrator, you could meet with central office administrators to discuss the district's teacher evaluation process. Not only will this provide an opportunity for professional dialogue, you will benefit from their experience. Similarly, if you are a veteran, you could consider asking other principals to meet together as a team and share copies of sample observation write-ups. The conversations that result will build collegiality while helping each team member enhance personal teacher evaluation skills.

Strategy 3: Be recognized as the most positive member of your administrative team.   With whom would you rather be a colleague, an administrator with a half-full or half-empty perspective? It is difficult to earn a reputation as a true team member when others feel uncomfortable around you. Those who are upbeat and positive can have a much stronger impact on others than those who tend to find fault or complain regularly. Superintendents want administrators who see possibilities, not just problems. They want leaders whom others respect, who can influence administrative team ideas, and who make a difference implementing initiatives.

Strategy 4: Volunteer to assist your administrative colleagues.   One of the most effective ways to demonstrate a commitment to the team is to offer to assist your colleagues. Such a simple gesture says volumes about you as a person. It also builds team relationships. Personnel responsibilities lend themselves well to collaboration. Whether you volunteer to assist principals with hiring, actively engage in district walk-throughs, or volunteer to serve on a teacher evaluation committee, others will view you as team-oriented.

One key to volunteering is taking the initiative rather than waiting to be asked. Contacting other principals or central office staff with an idea or even to offer to assist them is very effective. In fact, your efforts may be just what the district needs to push your entire administrative staff to collaborate at a higher level. In the process, you will enhance your reputation with your superintendent.

Strategy 5: Look for opportunities to evaluate teachers with a col-league.   Unless you are in a school with multiple administrators, you traditionally complete teacher evaluations yourself. However, if you share a faculty member between schools, you have the unique opportunity to team the evaluation. Rather than designating one of you to be the evaluator, suggest that you conduct the full evaluation as a team. This may be somewhat time consuming but will improve the thoroughness of the evaluation while connecting you with your colleague.

Strategy 6: Admit when you make a mistake.   Some administrators always have to be correct. They never let down their guards or admit that something they did was unsuccessful. Furthermore, if you mention an accomplishment, they are quick to tell how something they did was even more successful. These types of behaviors are counterproductive to building a closely knit administrative team.

The reality is that all administrators make mistakes, especially related to personnel. Have you ever hired a teacher whom you were convinced would be outstanding who proved troublesome? Have you ever taken a shortcut during the teacher evaluation process or failed to complete a required form? Those who say they have done everything correctly or tout their successes are quickly dismissed by colleagues as disingenuous.

Those who present themselves as unafraid to admit shortcomings tend to be respected for their honesty. Remember that your superinten-dent would much rather hear about a misstep immediately than from a board member or teacher later. Failing to inform central office adminis-trators is fraught with potential problems such as parents or teachers going over your head to the superintendent. Proactive communication will create closer bonds between you and other district administrators while helping to create more team-friendly relationships with your ad-ministrative colleagues.

Strategy 7: Seek out central office administrators' advice and assis-tance.   The success of superintendents and central office administrators is linked to that of their building-level administrators. Most district-level administrators want to do everything they can to support principals and assistant principals. As a result, rather than minimizing interactions with them, you should look for opportunities to tap their expertise, especially during the teacher hiring and supervision/evaluation processes. What you will discover is that most will relish the opportunity to be included. Just as important, they can alert you to potential issues and even political or legal landmines that you may not otherwise have considered.

At the same time, though, you should avoid overusing them as your resources. Similar to all administrators, their available time is limited. You should only seek their counsel if you truly need it. Do not equate the volume of communication you initiate with increased support. Over-communicating can actually hurt your relationships with central office administrators. It can also cause them to see you as too needy rather than independent. The key to this strategy is finding the proper balance between seeking their counsel and contacting them too often.

Strategy 8: Do not be afraid to offer dissenting opinions. Some administrators are reluctant to disagree with other team members, especially the superintendent. They choose to say nothing rather than share their honest opinions. This actually hurts the administrative team's productivity. The key is to disagree when you feel strongly but not be disagreeable. You must speak up if you have a concern to help the team properly consider all sides of any issue. Such team member interaction can often be the deciding factor in whether one of your colleagues or even your superintendent makes a sound decision.

Strategy 9: Fully disclose information you have about any internal or external teacher candidate. All administrators have information at one point or another about a person applying for a position or a transfer. Some administrators may choose to minimize potential problems or even give a mediocre performer a glowing report. Such actions are unethical and will lead to a loss of trust between you and your administrative colleagues. As a team player, you must fully disclose what you know even if it is not in your personal best interest.

Strategy 10: Never "poach" a teacher or other staff member from another school. All relationships are built on a foundation of trust. Once it begins to erode, it is very difficult to patch. As a consequence, never contact teachers or even secretaries from other schools, who you see as superior performers, about openings. If you are considering such an action, always talk with the person's principal first. If support is not there, you are better served not to proceed. However, sometimes these conversations lead to agreements among colleagues who may appreciate your position after your discussion.

Strategy 11: Inform your superintendent whenever you are contacted by board of education members about anything not related to their child's education. Exercising caution in your interactions with board members is good administrative practice. It is not uncommon for board members to ask principals how certain new teachers are performing or for them to offer their personal evaluations. Your superintendent can advise you on how best to handle such interactions as well as follow up as appropriate with board members.

Strategy 12: Be thorough. Whether you are hiring, supervising, or evaluating teachers, be thorough. You want to earn a reputation among your administrative colleagues as very conscientious. As day-to-day pressures mount, the temptation to take shortcuts can be strong. As the supervisor, you often have the latitude to decide, for example, how thoroughly you will check references or in how much depth you will evaluate each teacher. If you choose to do the minimum to satisfy district requirements, expect that over time your central office administrators and other building colleagues will note this. They may or may not question you about your thoroughness. However, they will become less confident in what you say and do.

To win their highest level of support and cement stronger team relationships, you must earn a reputation for thoroughness. If you work hard, fulfill all your personnel responsibilities, and demonstrate your competency, you will impress your district administrators. This support will help you foster much more productive relationships with them.

Strategy 13: Complete accurate teacher evaluations. No matter how thorough state or local contractual teacher evaluation requirements are, your teacher evaluations are only effective as they are accurate. Central office administrators and school board members expect that your teacher evaluations will be objective and reflect actual performance. Unfortunately, some administrators avoid both of these expectations. They sidestep parts of the process, complete very generic evaluations, or rate all teachers as excellent. In essence, they do not really evaluate them. Rather, they just go through the motions.

To earn the respect of your administrative team members, ensure that each teacher evaluation is linked directly to research-based observed teaching behavior. The Danielson Framework, which includes rubric-based comprehensive performance descriptors, is currently a popular model. Teacher evaluations today must be well grounded in observable behaviors, which are documented. The days of dropping in and making global judgments are long gone. Your central office administrators, boards of education, and teacher associations expect a much more sophisticated level of performance. The thoroughness of teacher evaluation has become increasingly important as administrators and school boards have gained broader authority to evaluate and even dismiss teachers.

If you fail to meet these increased teacher evaluation performance standards, your credibility as an evaluator and school leader will likely come under the microscope. If other administrators are rating teachers objectively while you skew yours toward excellent, you will quickly lose the respect and support of your colleagues. Once this occurs, reestablishing positive relationships with your district-level administrators will be difficult. Just as important, you will be viewed as a nonteam player.

POINTS TO REMEMBER

Functioning as a collaborative administrative team member is critical to your success. It is especially important when hiring, supervising, and evaluating teachers. To build positive relationships, you must be supportive of district decisions. You must also be positive and inclusive. Other team-building strategies include offering assistance and admitting when you make a mistake, as well as being thorough and ethical. By following these strategies, you can develop effective, collaborative relationships with your administrative team members.

Closing Thoughts

Although administrators have many responsibilities, none is more critical to the school, student, and their personal success than the hiring, supervision, and evaluation of teachers. The research evidence is clear. Excellent teachers make the difference in how well students achieve and how much schools improve. As such, is it any wonder that the most successful administrators make these personnel responsibilities their top priority?

If you hope to build the most outstanding faculty possible, you must begin by designing a comprehensive teacher selection processes. You should "leave no stone unturned" in your quest to hire the best teachers available. This process begins with maximizing your applicant pool. The larger the number of candidates you have to consider, the greater the likelihood that you will to select outstanding teachers.

In addition to maximizing your candidate pool, you must implement a well-structured and thorough selection process. This includes multiple layers of interviews designed to narrow a broad field of candidates to those you employ. Your goal through this process is to get to know each applicant as thoroughly as you can. If you do, you will be well positioned to make the most informed decisions possible. Through these interviews, which typically include other district administrators and often building faculty members, you hone in on candidates' knowledge of teaching and learning as well as their technology and communication skills. You also assess their ability to relate well with students and adults to determine their potential to be contributing faculty members.

As part of the selection process, you should also ensure that you observe your final candidates work directly with students. To accomplish this, build in a demonstration teaching component. If you use a modified clinical supervision process, you can observe them teach a short lesson as well as conference with them before and after the lesson. This will let you observe their natural teaching ability and see how they relate to you in a semi-supervisory environment.

Finally, you must do your due diligence. This means ensuring that you have thoroughly vetted each candidate who you are seriously considering. In addition to traditional reference checking, you should tap your professional network through informal contacts to learn as much as you can about each person. You never want to employ teachers without doing everything possible to get to know them well.

Once you have hired them, your job is not yet complete. You need to be sure that you build into your professional development plan both induction and mentoring programs. Through such programs, you can increase the likelihood that new faculty members will develop the knowledge and skill as well as receive the support they need to be successful.

In addition to providing new teachers with professional support, you are also responsible for their supervision and evaluation. How diligently and thoroughly you address both of these responsibilities will be critical to building and maintaining an outstanding school faculty.

Unlike even a few years ago, parents, boards of education, political leaders, and other stakeholders today are less willing to accept poor teaching, especially as teacher job protection rights have weakened. As a result, you will be required to be much more judgmental about teacher performance. You will be expected to either help teachers develop as professionals or dismiss them.

To meet these increased expectations, you will need to be very knowledgeable about the latest research-based teaching practices as well as teacher supervision and evaluation strategies. Without a thorough understanding of what teachers do to improve student learning, you will not be prepared to fully supervise and evaluate teachers for excellence.

This book, *Personnel Priorities in Schools Today: Hiring, Supervising, and Evaluating Teachers,* was designed to explore in-depth each of these three important administrative responsibilities. Discussed were key issues and emerging trends that impact the hiring, supervision, and teacher evaluation processes. Provided were a discussion of stumbling blocks to success as well as a plethora of practical strategies you could use to ensure that you hire, develop, and retain the most outstanding teachers possible. If you succeed in these areas, you will increase your effectiveness as the school's leader. Even more importantly, you will make a real difference in the quality of education each of your students receives.

References

Association for Effective Schools, Inc. (1996). *What is effective schools research?* Retrieved April 28, 2014, from http://www.mes.org/esr.html.

Baker, C. T. (1996). An historical perspective on teacher evaluation as a method of bureaucratic control. ProQuest 30474408, Dissertation 9716529, Ann Arbor, MI.

Berg, C. A., & Clough, M. (1990). Hunter lesson design: The wrong one for science teaching. *Educational Leadership*, 48(4), 73–78.

Beyer, B. M., & Johnson, E. S. (2005). *Special programs and services in schools: Creating options, meeting needs.* Lancaster, PA: Pro-Active Publications.

Burke, P. J., & Krey, R. D. (2005). *Supervision: A Guide to instructional leadership.* Springfield, IL: Charles C. Thomas Publisher.

Danielson, C. (2007). *Enhancing professional practice: A framework for teaching* (2nd ed.). Alexandria, VA: Association for Supervision and Curriculum Development (ASCD).

Danielson, C. (2012). Observing classroom practice. *Educational Leadership*, 70(3), 32–37.

Darling-Hammond, L. (2010, Oct.). *Evaluating teacher effectiveness: How teacher performance assessments can measure and improve teaching.* Retrieved from http://www.americanprogress.org/wp-content/uploads/issues/2010/10/pdf/teacher_effectiveness.pdf.

Educational Commission of the States. (1999). *Teacher tenure/continuing contract laws: Updated for 1998.* Retrieved November 1, 2006, from http://www.ecs.org/clearinghouse/14/41/1441.htm.

Fowler-Finn, T. (2014). Differentiating instructional rounds from walk-throughs. *School Administrator*, 71(1), 30–31.

Frey, D. (2010). *State teacher tenure/continuing contract laws.* Educational Commission of the States: StateNote. Retrieved November 15, 2013, from http://www/ecs.org/html/Document.asp?chouseid=8828.

Fullan, M. (1993). *Change forces.* Philadelphia, PA: Falmer Press.

Fullan, M. (2008). *The six secrets of change.* San Francisco: Jossey-Bass.

Garber, S. (2007). *Sputnik and the dawn of the space age.* Retrieved June 4, 2014, from http://history.nasa.gov/sputnik/index.html.

Goldrick, L., Osta, D., Barlin, D., & Burns, J. (2012, Feb.). *Review of state policies on teacher induction.* Retrieved June 7, 2014 from http://www.newteachercenter.org/sites/default/files/ntc/main/resources/brf-ntc-policy-state-teacher-induction.pdf.

Hattie, J. (2009). *Visible learning: A synthesis of over 800 meta-analyses relating to achievement.* New York: Routledge, Taylor & Francis Group.

Hunter, M. (1982). *Mastery teaching.* Thousand Oaks, CA: Corwin Press.

Huvaere, D. J. (1997). Tenure for Illinois teachers: An analysis of the philosophical arguments surrounding the adoption of the 1941 Tenure law for public school teachers in the state of Illinois. Doctoral dissertation, Loyola University Chicago, 1997. *Dissertation Abstracts International*, 58 (0), 777 (AAT 9726387).

Independence Hall Association. (2013). *Economic growth and the early industrial revolution.* Retrieved March 28, 2014, from http://www.ushistory.org.us/22a.asp.

Kersten, T. A. (2006). Teacher tenure: Illinois school board presidents' perspectives and suggestions for improvement. *Planning and Changing*, 37(3 & 4), 234–257.

Kersten, T. A. (2010). *Stepping into administration: How to succeed in making the move.* Lanham, MD: Rowman & Littlefield Education.

Kersten, T. A., & Ballenger, J. (2012). School and district relationships. In Acker-Hocevar, M. A., Ballenger, J., Place, A. W., & Ivory, G., *Snapshots of school leadership in the 21st century: Perils and promises of leading for social justice, school improvement, and democratic community*. Charlotte, NC: Information Age Publishing.

Kram, K. (1983). Phases of the mentor relationship. *Academy of Management Journal, 26*(4), 608–625.

Marshall, K. (2012). Fine-tuning teacher evaluation. *Educational Leadership, 70*(3), 50–53.

Marzano, R. J. (2012).The two purposes of teacher evaluation. *Educational Leadership, 70*(3), 14–19.

Marzano, R. J., Frontier, T., & Livingston, D. (2011). *Effective supervision: Supporting the art and science of teaching 2011*. Alexandria, VA: Association for Supervision and Curriculum Development.

Marzano R. J., Waters, J. T., & McNulty, B. A. (2005). *School leadership that works: From research to results*. Alexandria, VA: Association for Supervision and Curriculum Development.

McGreal, T. L. (1983). *Successful teacher evaluation*, Alexandria, VA: Association for Supervision and Curriculum Development.

Moir, E. (2011). *Phases of first-year teaching*. Retrieved June 7, 2014, from http://www.newteachercenter.org/blog/phases-first-year-teaching.

Moss, C. M., & Brookhart, S. M. (2013). A new view of walk-throughs. *Educational Leadership, 70*(7), 42–45.

National Commission on Excellence in Education. (1983). *A nation at risk*. Retrieved April 28, 2014, from http://www2.ed.gov/pubs/NatAtRisk/risk.html.

National Education Association Alaska. (2005). *Teacher tenure: Frequently asked questions*. Retrieved November 1, 2006, from http://www.ak.nea.org/formembers/tenure_faq.htm.

National Governors Association Center for Best Practices, Council of Chief State School Officers. (2010). *Common core state standards*. National Governors Association Center for Best Practices, Council of Chief State School Officers, Washington, DC.

Nettles, S. M., & Herrington, C. (2007). Revisiting the importance of the direct effects of school leadership on student achievement: The implications for school policy. *Peabody Journal of Education, 82*(4), 724–736.

Sarason, S. B. (1993). *The case for change: Rethinking the preparation of educators*. San Francisco: Josssey-Bass.

Taylor, F. E. (1911). *The principles of scientific management*. Reprinted 2007. Sioux Falls, SD: NuVision.

Tracy, S. (1995). How historical concepts of supervision relate to supervisory practices today. *The Clearing House, 68*(5), 320–324.

Tucker P. D., & Stronge, J. H. (2005). *Linking teacher evaluation and student learning*. Alexandria, VA: Association for Supervision and Curriculum Development.

U.S. Department of Education. (2013). *ED.GOV National Blue Ribbon Schools Program*. Retrieved September 20, 2013, from http://www2.ed.gov/programs/nclbbrs/index.html.

About the Authors

Thomas A. Kersten is associate professor emeritus in educational leadership at Roosevelt University in Chicago and Schaumburg, Illinois. He has twenty-eight years of public school administrative experience in Illinois including eleven as superintendent. He is also the author of *Stepping into Administration: How to Succeed in Making the Move* and *Moving into the Superintendency: How to Succeed in Making the Transition*.

Margaret E. Clauson is currently assistant superintendent in Wilmette, Illinois. She has served as an Illinois educator for over twenty years as a teacher, assistant principal, middle school principal, administrator for human resources, and assistant superintendent. She has written and presented on a variety of leadership topics.

Lightning Source UK Ltd.
Milton Keynes UK
UKHW010612240519
343219UK00001B/271/P